British Universities

SIR JAMES MOUNTFORD

British Universities

W 99

London
OXFORD UNIVERSITY PRESS
New York Toronto
1966

Oxford University Press, Ely House, London W.1

GLASGOW NEW YORK TORONTO MELBOURNE WELLINGTON
CAPE TOWN SALISBURY IBADAN NAIROBI LUSAKA ADDIS ABABA
BOMBAY CALCUTTA MADRAS KARACHI LAHORE DACCA
KUALA LUMPUR HONG KONG

PRINTED IN GREAT BRITAIN BY
HAZELL WATSON AND VINEY LTD, AYLESBURY, BUCKS

TO DORIS

_____

Contents

Note 1 : The following abbreviations are used
CATS: *Colleges of Advanced Technology (see p. 43)*
DES: *The Department of Education and Science (see p. 73)*
LEA: *Local Education Authority (see p. 44)*
Robbins: *Report of the Committee on Higher Education
     (chairman, Lord Robbins; issued in 1963) (see p. 41)*
UGC: *The University Grants Committee (see p. 152)*

Note 2: Complete statistics for sessions later than
1963–4 were not available when this book was
written

1
Historical Outline

Introduction

KNOWLEDGE AT THE HIGHEST LEVEL is the domain of universities; their function is to preserve it, hand it on, and expand it. This is inherent in their nature and confirmed by their history. The relative emphasis on these three aspects of their work as the handmaids of truth has necessarily varied from age to age; for universities are part of the society in which they function and they are only viable if they respond, in ways consonant with their nature, to the implied needs and the positive demands of changing cultural, social, economic, and political environments. Wisdom they may foster, but cannot teach; and though not indifferent to the training of character, they must in the main regard it as a prior responsibility of home, church, and school. The knowledge with which they are concerned is that which is ascertainable by human reason and observation; prophecy and revelation are outside their orbit, though theology is not. Their attitude is of necessity critical; they tend to be radical rather than conservative; they are seminaries for new ideas and a sanctuary for unpopular opinion; freedom of thought and expression is essential to their existence.

In practical terms universities are communities of those who teach and those who learn, places where the minds of maturing students are trained and strengthened and where the future leaders in a society are prepared not only for the learned professions and tasks of responsibility in the community, but also for the living of a full life. No less importantly universities are places where by reappraisal and original investigations new additions are continuously being made to the sum of human knowledge and understanding.

The British universities at the present time have entered on a period of expansion, development, and reorganization unprecedented in their history; since 1945 the number of institutions of university status has almost doubled and the enrolment of students has increased almost fourfold; what the universities do and how they do it have become topics of general interest to the community at large. It is the purpose of the following pages to describe these activities with as much factual detail as seems necessary and against an historical background which it is hoped will be illuminating.

Mediaeval universities

The spirit of inquiry and the tradition of learning originating with the Greeks, fostered by Alexandria, and transmitted by Rome, never entirely died out in Europe even in the darkest ages. The Church took over the task of education from an expiring paganism and the torch of learning was kept alight, however dimly, in the schools associated with cathedrals, abbeys, and monasteries. Scarcely any century was without some scholars of eminence: England can claim men of European stature in Bede of Jarrow (673–735), Alcuin of York (735–804) and John of Salisbury (1115–1180). The twelfth century saw an exceptional efflorescence of scholarship and of theological and philosophical disputation. For this there were two main reasons: a wider dissemination of the writings of Aristotle in Latin translations, and a revival of interest in Roman law.

It was in the twelfth and early thirteenth centuries that the earliest universities in Europe came into being. Exact dates cannot be given in many cases for their foundation: they had some kind of existence many years before a papal Bull was issued in their favour. It happened that at a number of places—Paris, Bologna, Salerno, Montpellier, Orleans—the presence of outstanding teachers like Peter Abelard (1079–1142) at Paris and Irnerius (c. 1075–1140) at Bologna, attracted students from far afield and a centre of learning grew up. One place might be particularly notable in arts, philosophy, and theology like Paris, another in law like Bologna and Orleans, another in medicine like Salerno and Montpellier; and because each centre drew students from all parts of Europe it was called a *studium generale*.

In an age when crafts and trades were beginning to organize themselves in guilds, it was natural for groups of teachers and students to form associations for mutual protection against exploitation by townsfolk and for their own self-government. Inevitably it was to the Church that, as places of learning, the *studia generalia* turned for legal confirmation by papal Bull of the status and privileges they sought. A common mediaeval term for any association of people in their corporate capacity was *universitas*, 'the corporation', 'all of you'. The word did not then specifically imply that the group or guild was concerned with learning; but it was freely used alongside *studium generale* and eventually superseded it. Generally it was the teachers who obtained recognition as a *universitas magistrorum*; but notably at Bologna it was the students who prevailed as a *universitas scholarium*. At one period there were actually four separate *universitates* recognized at Bologna and Montpellier, corresponding to what we should now call faculties in arts, law, medicine, and theology.

Education in the mediaeval university was based on the 'seven liberal arts' consisting of the *trivium* (grammar, rhetoric, and logic) and the *quadrivium* (arithmetic, geometry, astronomy, and music—the latter being theoretical and really a branch of mathematics). Students began their studies at an early age—fourteen or even younger—and proceeded by well-defined stages, steps (*gradus*), or 'degrees'. After entering his name on the roll (*matricula*) of a master, a student spent four years or so before his first test or 'determination' in the subjects of the *trivium*, success in which made him a 'bachelor'. He now had an adequate knowledge of Latin and had learned the art of discussion and debate. A further four years of study in the subjects of the *quadrivium* and the three philosophies (natural, moral, and metaphysical) led to his 'inception' as a 'master' and the grant of a *licentia* which gave him the right to teach anywhere (*ius ubique docendi*). Beyond this there were, for the relatively few, the three higher faculties of law, medicine, and theology, and it might be another six to ten years before the student, now a mature man and often a beneficed priest, was thought worthy to be admitted to the degree of 'doctor'.

The university, though having a corporate existence, did not for a long time possess buildings or revenues of its own, and lectures, for which students paid the masters a fee, were given in hired halls. The students themselves also were poor, ill-disciplined, and often riotous; many stayed only for a year or two. They lived as best they could in lodgings, but sometimes on a partly communal basis in a hostel under the direction of a master. In some places students were organized in 'nations' according to the country of their origin. Migration of individual students and sometimes even of teachers from one university to another was frequent and the use of Latin as the universal language of instruction made such transfers easy. Occasionally dissatisfaction with the townsfolk or a conflict within the university led to a large and concerted exodus and a resettlement elsewhere.

Oxford and Cambridge

The most credible account of the origin of the University of Oxford connects it with the year 1167 when Henry II in the course of his quarrel with Thomas à Becket placed an embargo on English clerks going abroad. Students and teachers who were thus forced to return from the University of Paris chose Oxford as the place to settle and establish a new *studium*. The earliest known grant of privileges dates from the formal recognition of Oxford by a papal legate in 1214. Cambridge had its origin in the migration of a group of teachers and students from Oxford in 1209. The university there was well enough established for Henry III to intervene in 1231 to regulate the rent of lodgings, and in 1318, at the request of Edward II, its rights and privileges were confirmed by a papal Bull of John XXII.

It is only the briefest summary that can here be given of the history of two great universities extending over nearly eight centuries. Broadly, three periods may be conveniently distinguished: the first to 1500, the second to about 1800, and the third to the present day. During their first three centuries Oxford and Cambridge did not differ essentially from other mediaeval universities in organization or curriculum. Thanks in part to the scholarly influence of Franciscan and other friars who settled in the universities in the thirteenth century, both established themselves—but Oxford the more rapidly—as centres of learning respected all over Europe in arts, philosophy, and theology. But this early period was far from being a time of tranquil progress. There was much internal disharmony; in 1263, for example, there was a secession from Oxford to Northampton, and a more serious one in 1334 to Stamford. Discipline was difficult to maintain. Cambridge insisted from 1276 that every scholar should be under the care of a master; and matters improved only slowly as colleges were founded. There were also bitter and continuous quarrels with the townsfolk, which frequently resulted in violence, riots, bloodshed, and murder. The universities, however, could rely on Church and king to support them and eventually gained for themselves a firm grip over civic affairs, including the right of their elected chancellor to try all cases in which a scholar was involved. There were conflicts too with ecclesiastical authority: Oxford disputed the claims of the Bishop of Lincoln and Cambridge those of the Bishop of Ely to exercise control.

The second period begins at the turn of the fifteenth and sixteenth centuries when the influence of the Renaissance was making itself felt in England. The tortuously elaborate synthesis of Aristotelian philosophy and Christian theology which goes under the name of scholasticism slowly lost its hold. Greek began to be taught (by Erasmus in Cambridge, and by Grocyn, Linacre, Colet, and More at Oxford) and the wider outlook of the Italian humanists permeated both universities. The Reformation brought its difficulties. The confiscations arising from the dissolution of the monasteries affected the revenues of the universities and the colleges, though some religious houses were refounded as colleges, like Magdalene at Cambridge. Henry VIII forbade the teaching of canon law in the universities but made some amends by founding several 'Regius' chairs. During the Marian persecutions, three Cambridge divines, Latimer, Ridley, and (later) Cranmer, were burned at the stake in Oxford. Elizabeth I was well disposed to the universities, regarding them as bulwarks of Church and state alike. Her Act of 1571 remodelled their constitutions and concentrated power in the heads of colleges. Her statutes for Cambridge prevailed for well over two hundred years, but those made for Oxford were superseded by the 1636 statutes of Archbishop Laud. During the Civil War both universities were largely royalist and for a time Oxford was actually the headquarters of the King. There followed a sad period of intellectual decline: professors were often grossly ignorant of the subjects they were appointed to teach, college tutors were indolent, and the students, now drawn mostly from the gentry, spent their time in idleness and sometimes in dissolute living. It was only in the second half of the eighteenth century that there was an awakening, notably in Cambridge where mathematical studies became established (until 1850) as a compulsory part of the curriculum.

The third period, and particularly the nineteenth century, was an age of reform. 'Tripos' examinations were instituted at Cambridge in classics (1824), natural science (1851), law (1859), and history (1870). From 1800 similar honours schools were inaugurated in Oxford; and the school of *literae humaniores* or 'Greats', involving the study of ancient history and philosophy on a basis of the classics, acquired great prestige as a broad training which fitted a man for any post of administrative responsibility. Parties of reform in both universities urged and obtained the appointment of royal commissions; and the resulting Acts of Parliament (1854, 1856, 1877, and last of all 1923) transformed the administration of the universities. College scholarships, which had been closed to particular schools, localities, dioceses, or even the kin of the founder, were thrown open for competition; Oriel College at Oxford led the way in opening its fellowships to competition; religious tests were abolished; the range of studies was widened; and by stages women were given the same status as men.

What, above all else, is characteristic of Oxford and Cambridge is the collegiate system, which dates back to the Middle Ages. The earliest of the colleges were founded within the first century of the existence of the universities. At Oxford a bequest made by William of Durham (d. 1249) to the university to support ten masters led to the establishment of University College. About 1260 John Balliol gave money as an act of penance to maintain scholars; and in 1264 Walter de Merton founded a college for 20 scholars. At Cambridge the oldest college, Peterhouse, was founded in 1284 by Hugo de Balsham, Bishop of Ely, on the model of Merton. It is an indication of the growing importance of the universities that many of the later foundations were due to royal patronage. In the fourteenth century four colleges were founded at Oxford (Exeter, Oriel, Queen's, and New College) and five at Cambridge (Clare, Pembroke, Gonville and Caius, Trinity Hall, and Corpus). New College in Oxford was established in 1379 by William de Wykeham as a sister to his foundation at Winchester and the close connexion between the school and the college has persisted to the present day. In the fifteenth century three colleges were founded at Oxford (Lincoln, All Souls, and Magdalen) and four at Cambridge (King's, Queens', St. Catharine's, and Jesus). All Souls was established for masters, and it still has no undergraduates; its roll of fellows includes men of outstanding eminence; and the winning of one of its competitive fellowships is widely regarded as the high-water mark of academic distinction. King's at Cambridge was founded in 1441 by Henry VI as a sister to Eton, and until 1861 did not admit scholars from any other school. In the sixteenth century the two most notable foundations were: Christ Church at Oxford, which was projected by Cardinal Wolsey in 1525 and finally established by Henry VIII in 1546; and Trinity College at Cambridge, which Henry VIII refounded as an amalgamation of two previously existing hostels.

In the intervening centuries other colleges have been founded, but there were no colleges for women until the nineteenth century. Of special interest are: Nuffield College, Oxford founded in 1937 by a great philanthropist, mainly for post-graduate research in social studies and designed to foster the co-operation of academic and non-academic workers in those fields; St. Antony's, Oxford, founded in 1950 by a French benefactor for postgraduate studies in modern subjects and to provide a college for foreign students; and Churchill College at Cambridge, founded in 1960 as a tribute to a great statesman for the encouragement mainly of science and technology, es-pecially at the postgraduate level. There are now at Oxford 24 colleges for men, 5 for women, 2 for men and women, and 5 recognized 'halls' for men. At Cambridge there are 20 colleges for men and one recognized 'house'; for women there are 2 colleges and 2 recognized 'halls'.

The founding of colleges was not an idea peculiar to Oxford and Cambridge; there were colleges in all mediaeval univer-sities. At Paris, for example, there were not less than fifty and one of them, the Sorbonne, founded about 1255 for 'poor masters of theology', became so famous that its name is now a synonym for the University of Paris itself. But none of these colleges persisted, as they did in England, as residential insti-tutions providing teaching. The reason seems to be that the English colleges were better endowed, their deeds of founda-tion were more carefully and elaborately drawn and so ensured the continued existence of the colleges, and—what is of par-ticular importance—the masters in the colleges took the teach-ing into their own hands. The modern form of a college is that there is a head (variously called the Master, President, Principal, Provost, Rector or Warden) and a number of 'fellows' and 'scholars': all these are 'on the foundation' and receive emoluments from the college. It was not until the sixteenth century that colleges began to admit to their society other people who paid fees for the privilege of living and being taught there. These other members of the college are 'com-moners' or 'pensioners' and they now form the great major-ity. An important concomitant of the college system has been the development of the tutorial method of instruction in which

Oxford and Cambridge excel; but more will be said about this later.

The universities of Oxford and Cambridge are older than any of the colleges and it is misleading to think of them as federations of colleges. Each university has its own existence apart from the colleges, it provides some of the teaching, it alone examines and awards degrees, it must concur in any proposed change in the statutes of a college, and no new college can be founded without its sanction. At the same time the colleges have their own very considerable autonomies. They are self-perpetuating and elect their own fellows entirely at their discretion, they own and have absolute control over their own property, they manage their own finances, and, subject to the matriculation regulations of the university, they admit what students they please. Some of them are very wealthy indeed, though others now receive some help from the university's central funds. From the end of the sixteenth century to the middle of the nineteenth they overshadowed the university in every way, and a few dominant colleges determined university policy. The need, however, to make central provision for scientific subjects had a decisive effect in restoring the power of the university and the constitutional changes introduced by the nineteenth-century Acts of Parliament have given it once again a position of ultimate control.

It is not because of their antiquity, or the architectural charm and magnificence of many of their buildings, or the gracious amenities of college quadrangles, gardens, and lawns, but because of their achievements in learning in so many fields that these two universities are ranked amongst the greatest in the world. For five hundred years they were the only two universities in England, and it was inevitable that within their precincts many of our most distinguished statesmen, lawyers, men of letters, poets, scientists, and religious leaders should have received their education. The traditions thus founded and handed on are part of our national heritage. The heads and many of the fellows of colleges have been and continue to be men of great influence, having access to the seats of government. Faithful and grateful *alumni* have left bequests to the universities and the colleges, and because of their unrivalled prestige benefactions have been showered upon them from all parts of the world. In the main they attract the best students and the best staff; and whatever loyalties members of other universities may feel towards their own institutions, they could not in fairness deny that Oxford and Cambridge stand preeminent.

Scotland

IN HISTORIC SEQUENCE it is the universities of Scotland which must next be mentioned; for three of them were mediaeval foundations, and a fourth was established two hundred and fifty years before a third university came into being south of the border.

St. Andrews is the oldest of these Scottish universities. It was in 1410 that Henry Wardlaw, Bishop of St. Andrews, who had studied arts at Paris and law at Orleans, granted a charter for a university in that city on the model of Paris, to teach arts, theology, and canon law; and in 1413 he obtained a confirmatory Bull from Pope Benedict XIII. Hitherto Scottish students had in the main gone to John Balliol's college in Oxford, or to the Scots' college (1326) in Paris, or to Orleans and Padua where they had a recognized standing as a distinctive group or 'nation'. But at the end of the century the uneasy relations between England and Scotland, and the wavering allegiance of France in the matter of the rival Popes during the Great Schism, created difficulties for Scottish students; Bishop Wardlaw's new foundation in their own country provided a welcome alternative to residence abroad. A college, St. Salvator's, was founded and endowed in 1450, and the hospital of St. Leonard's became a college for needy scholars in 1512; but in 1747 St. Leonard's was merged with St. Salvator's, by which latter name the united college is now known. A third college, St. Mary's, founded in 1537 with a special interest in theology, still retains its identity. Situated in a city unaffected by the main streams of commerce and industry, St. Andrews is now the smallest of the Scottish universities. Most of its students come from outside its immediate area and in recent times it was the first of the universities north of the border to take seriously the need to provide residential accommodation for undergraduates.

Glasgow. A graduate of St. Andrews, William Turnbull, Bishop of Glasgow, in 1451 induced James II of Scotland to obtain from Pope Nicholas V a Bull establishing a university in that city. This new foundation, entitled to 'the privileges and exemptions of Bologna', was intended to provide for studies in arts, theology, and canon and civil law. But progress was fitful, and until after the Reformation it was only the faculty of arts that had a serious existence; there was a dearth of endowments, and though there were plans for colleges, none was permanently established. Under the energetic principalship of Andrew Melville, a new charter of James VI reconstituted the university in 1577. Thereafter it flourished with few interruptions. Its present size and importance can be related in large part to the growth of the port of Glasgow and the industrialization of the Clyde valley.

Aberdeen was the latest of the mediaeval universities to be established in Scotland. It was founded in 1494 by William Elphinstone, the local bishop and a graduate of Glasgow, Paris, and Orleans, who obtained a Bull from Pope Alexander VI through the intervention of James IV. Its main aim was to be the study of law and 'the promoting of civilization among the Highland clergy'. The renowned Hector Boece was brought from Paris to be the first principal, and Aberdeen speedily acquired great repute as a centre of learning. St. Mary's College—later known as King's College—was founded in 1505 and provided teachers in several faculties. But a rival institution came into existence in 1593 when George Keith, the fifth earl marischal, founded Marischal College on a distinctively Presbyterian basis; and a charter empowering it to confer degrees was ratified by an Act of the Scots Parliament. King's and Marischal existed as separate institutions until they were finally amalgamated by an Act of 1860 as the University of Aberdeen.

Edinburgh owes nothing to episcopal patronage and foresight. Despite the fact that the city was the capital and the headquarters of the Church and of the legal profession, it was not until 1583 that the town council itself founded the 'tounis colledge' with power to confer degrees under a general charter of James VI. In 1621, by an 'act of confirmation', this 'College of James VI', as it was also called, was formally granted such rights, privileges, and immunities as were enjoyed by the other three Scottish universities, and came to be known as the University of Edinburgh. For over two centuries, however, it remained firmly under the control of the town council, which jealously exercised its own rights, including the important one of making all appointments to professorships. In 1858, together with the other Scottish universities, it was reconstituted under an Act of Parliament.

The three oldest of the Scottish universities retained much of the pattern of the mediaeval curriculum almost as long as Oxford and Cambridge; but they never fell into such troughs of intellectual sloth as did the older universities of England in the seventeenth and eighteenth centuries. As a nation the Scots were keen for education, hard-working, and not prone even to the minor indulgences. The students were poor; and when the mediaeval custom of the 'common table' fell into disuse, the bag of oatmeal they brought with them from home often had to suffice for their main sustenance during the term. They were spurred on by the opportunities for advancement which their university training ensured for them, and their mentors too took their teaching duties seriously. This tradition of grim dedication to the acquisition of knowledge implanted itself also in the younger university in Edinburgh. Until quite recently, seven subjects had to be passed for the ordinary degree in Scotland, and the breadth of this curriculum, in which philosophy was rigorously embedded, gave a special quality to the Scottish graduate. The success and influence of the *alumni* of the Scottish universities in many spheres of national life is notorious; what is perhaps less well appreciated is the prominent part played in the development of younger universities, both in England and overseas, by professors and teachers who had received their education in the universities of Scotland.

A few years ago what has just been written would have closed the roll of Scottish universities; but there are now four new-comers.

Strathclyde was the first of these. Its origin goes back to 1796, when a college was founded in Glasgow for the study of scientific knowledge and its practical application, under the will of John Anderson, who for thirty-nine years had been pro-fessor of natural philosophy in the University of Glasgow. During the nineteenth century this college joined with or absorbed two similar institutions, and in 1913, when it had already become the Royal Technical College, it was affiliated with the University of Glasgow. Its standing was such that as early as 1919, although it had no power to award degrees, it was placed on the list of institutions of university rank to receive Treasury grants. Always independently minded, it was never fully incorporated within the university, and eventually in 1964 it received its own charter as the University of Strath-clyde.

Heriot-Watt. This second university in Edinburgh stems from a school of arts established in 1821 which later veered to scientific and practical subjects and assumed the title of Heriot-Watt in 1885. In recognition of its high standing in techno-logical education and research, it was affiliated to the Univer-sity of Edinburgh in 1933; and, in accordance with the pro-posals of the Robbins Committee, a charter granting indepen-dent university status was approved in 1966.

Dundee. In 1897 University College, which had been founded in Dundee under a trust deed in 1881, became affiliated with the University of St. Andrews. In 1898 the two institutions conjointly established a medical school in Dundee; in the other faculties some departments were wholly in St. Andrews, some were wholly in Dundee, while still others had sections in both places. But the relations between the college and the university were very often strained and sometimes deplorably bitter. The University of St. Andrews Act of 1953, by which (among other provisions) University College and the medical school were amalgamated as Queen's College, disposed of many of the causes of friction. By 1964, however, it was generally agreed that the time was ripe for Queen's College to be accorded full university status, and it is expected to receive its charter as the University of Dundee in 1967.

Stirling. The Robbins Committee recommended that there should be at least one new university in Scotland, and in 1964 it was decided at government level that such a university should be at Stirling. This location was deliberately chosen after consideration of claims from a number of towns in various parts of Scotland which were willing and eager to provide sites and financial backing. It is likely to receive its charter in 1967.

Many constitutional procedures, especially those affecting entrance requirements and the award of degrees, in the four older universities of Scotland were, until recently, regulated by two Acts of Parliament of 1858 and 1889, under which the four universities were bound to take counsel together. Mutual tolerance and common sense made this statutory fetter much less irksome than it might have been. The four new universities, however, are not to be tied by any such obligation to each other or to their older sisters, and the two Acts needed amending if the older universities were to enjoy as much individual freedom as the new. The necessary modifications were made by an Act of 1966, and new charters are envisaged for each of the four older universities.

London, Durham, and Newcastle

It is one of the curiosities of educational history that London had no university of its own before the nineteenth century; and no less curious are the origins and early years of that university. It was not that the capital was intellectually dormant: the Inns of Court dated from mediaeval times; the Royal Society was established in 1660, the Royal Institution in 1779; and many other cultural and learned associations proliferated widely. Yet no kind of rival to Oxford and Cambridge emerged until 1826. In that year an energetic group of persons headed by Lord

Brougham and Thomas Campbell, the poet, set up in Gower Street a 'University of London' (now University College), not by charter, but mundanely as a joint-stock enterprise. Apart from feeling that London ought to have a university of its own, the promoters were moved by resentment at the denominational tests which excluded dissenters and others from the two old universities, and by the fact that only the wealthier classes could afford to send their sons there.

The setting up of the 'godless' institution, which excluded theology and was not residential, called forth an immediate reaction. The Archbishop of Canterbury, the Prime Minister (the Duke of Wellington), and Sir Robert Peel led a movement which resulted in the foundation in 1829 by royal charter of King's College in the Strand, on a resolutely Anglican basis. Neither of the two new institutions, however, had the power to award degrees and it was this disability which led in 1836 to the establishment, again by royal charter, of the University of London itself. Yet, contrary to all tradition and precedent, the university was given no teaching function at all. Its sole powers were to examine and confer degrees on students attending approved institutions in the United Kingdom, including the two colleges already existing in London. It was indeed the colleges, not the university, which made a university education a reality in London. From 1849 any institution in the British Empire became eligible to be approved, and in 1858 even the requirement of actual attendance at an approved institution (except in medicine) was dropped. In this way the London 'external' degree was fully launched. Purists might raise their eyebrows at such an academic anomaly; but at this point of time we can appreciate how important was to be the role played by this degree. It served as a stimulus for the maintenance of standards in university colleges in other parts of the country; it was the goal and honourable reward of many thousands of eager students who attended evening classes (if they could find any), or paid for correspondence courses, or toiled arduously on their own: they missed much that is important in a university education, but their academic achievement at least was recognized; and it was within the general pattern of this external degree that the University of London was uniquely able from 1945 onwards to discharge the urgent task of fostering the development of colleges and embryonic universities overseas: in the West Indies, the Gold Coast, Nigeria, East Africa, the Sudan, and Rhodesia and Nyasaland.

In 1898, and again in 1926, Acts of Parliament revised the constitution of the university, and amongst other things empowered it to give instruction as well as to examine; consequently, by drawing on the resources of its constituent colleges, the university itself now organizes an appreciable amount of centralized teaching, particularly in honours and postgraduate courses. Furthermore, the relationships between the colleges in London and the university were clarified within the framework of a federal constitution which, despite its forbidding complexities, has been made to work. The colleges, while having a status as 'schools' of the university, enjoy a great measure of freedom, especially as regards selection of students, the control of their own teaching, and the drawing up of the syllabuses for internal students. As a result of comments made in the Robbins Report, a number of academic and administrative reforms are being considered by the university and the colleges. Whether some of the colleges or groups of colleges will petition for a charter of their own as separate universities, or whether the present federal structure can be so modified as to remove all major objections and satisfy all reasonable claims: these are matters awaiting decisions.

London is now the largest university in the country; in 1963–4 it had 23,955 full-time students and by 1966 the number had risen to 26,454. It embraces 13 medical schools associated with teaching hospitals, 2 postgraduate medical schools, 14 non-medical colleges, and a number of other postgraduate and special institutions which are the direct responsibility of the university. In addition, some other institutions of higher education in London are affiliated with the university, and in still others a number of members of staff are recognized as teachers of the university. Ten of the 13 medical schools are older than the university: the schools at St. George's, Guy's, and the London Hospital go back to the eighteenth century; St.

Thomas's Hospital traces its origins to the thirteenth, and St. Bartholomew's to the twelfth century. Some of the non-medical colleges, notably University, King's, the Imperial College of Science and Technology, St. Mary's College, and the London School of Economics, rank with independent universities in the number of their undergraduate and post-graduate students and in academic distinction. Three of the colleges (Bedford, Royal Holloway, and Westfield) were until recently exclusively for women. Taken as a whole, the constituent colleges and institutes cover a wider range of studies than any other university in the country.

Durham. Cromwell had established a college in Durham in 1656, but it was abolished at the Restoration. The present university was founded in 1832 and had its origin in the Anglican principles, the political fears, and the worldly shrewdness of the wealthy cathedral Chapter. Disapproval of the secular nature of University College, London, was as keenly felt in Durham as in the metropolis; even more alarming to the Chapter were the radical ideas of the time which found expression in the 1832 Reform Bill: would it not be prudent of the Chapter to avoid the risk of having their great revenues confiscated by diverting part of them to an undeniably worthy purpose, such as the founding of a university, which would serve God and thwart Mammon? These ambivalent designs were brought to final fruition by a charter of 1837. Oxford and Cambridge were to be the models for the new university; it was to be on a collegiate pattern and its emphasis was to be on arts and divinity. The first college (University) was founded in 1833 and housed in Durham Castle, which is still its home. Other colleges followed, including St. Mary's for women (1899); and until 1946 all students at Durham resided in a college. The teaching, however, is organized centrally. The first narrow concept of the curriculum did not prevail; engineering studies were soon introduced, and a strong scientific side developed rapidly.

Newcastle. Thirty miles north of Durham, in Newcastle-upon-Tyne, the financial help of local industrialists made possible the founding in 1871, as part of the university, of the Durham College of Physical Science, which from 1904 was better known as Armstrong College. In Newcastle also, a college of medicine and surgery, dating from 1834, had already come into association with the university in 1852 and still more closely in 1870. This medical college and Armstrong College became amalgamated in 1937 as King's College. The university was thus harmoniously organized on a quasi-federal basis in two divisions, one in Durham, the other in Newcastle, each having its own council and academic board and controlling its own teaching. The university senate had responsibility for degree examinations, and the vice-chancellor-ship was held in rotation, for two years each, by the academic heads of the two divisions. By 1960, however, King's College had become one of the larger institutions in the country; and it was with the unqualified goodwill of the Durham division that Newcastle obtained a charter in 1963 as a separate university. The constitutions of both Durham and Newcastle now closely resemble those of the civic universities.

The civic universities

Twelve universities are grouped under this heading. In the order in which they were granted their charters constituting them as autonomous universities with power to award their own degrees, they are as follows: Manchester (1880), Birmingham (1900), Liverpool (1903), Leeds (1904), Sheffield (1905), Bristol (1909), Reading (1926), Nottingham (1948), Southampton (1952), Hull (1954), Exeter (1955), and Leicester (1957). Between the opening in 1851 of Owens College, from which the University of Manchester developed, and the granting of a charter to Leicester in 1957, there intervened the most important century in the history of British education, a century which saw the passing of the Education Acts of 1870, 1902, 1918, and 1944, and the remarkable progress from the first organization of compulsory elementary education to the provision of free secondary education for all and a statutory leaving age of 15, soon to be raised to 16.

During those hundred years, these twelve universities and the institutions from which they grew played a crucial role in the diffusion of higher education. Situated as they are in large centres of population throughout the country, they kindled and held aloft the torch of scientific and humane learning despite daunting difficulties. In parts of the country far removed from the two old universities and the metropolis, with a quiet and determined patience they established and have continuously maintained those standards of intellectual achievement without which no national system of education has a true and final touchstone; and they have in consequence made a major contribution to the supply of people of the quality—and in the numbers—which a developed twentieth-century society demands and without which it could not survive. Through their classrooms and laboratories there have passed generation after generation of eager and talented students, for whom, until 1945, expense and not lack of ability made Oxford and Cambridge inaccessible. From them have come leaders in the church and the learned professions, in science and the arts, in politics, and in commerce and industry; and many others who hold positions of influence in all walks of life. Without the graduates they produced, the grammar schools set up under the 1902 Act could not have found sufficient men and women to impart the instruction required. In expanding the scope of university interest to include new subjects—engineering, metallurgy, architecture, veterinary science, radiology, psychiatry, accountancy, and industrial management spring readily to mind—it was often they who took the first steps or initiated major developments. It is these universities which have borne, and for some time to come are likely to bear, the brunt of the post-war expansions in numbers. In 1938–9 they had about 11,500 full-time students, which was almost one-third of the total of university students in England; by 1963–4 their numbers had risen to 45,531, which was almost half of that total; by 1966 the figure had again risen to 53,737; and the plans for implementing the Robbins Report depend upon a still further significant increase in their student population.

It was once customary to refer to these universities as 'provincial' or 'modern'; and Bruce Truscot's astringent *Red Brick University* (1943) gave currency to the term 'redbrick', which brutally distinguishes them from the older universities which Thackeray had compendiously referred to as 'Oxbridge' or 'Camford'. But the derogatory overtones which all these epithets for the civic universities have acquired and the difficulty of finding parallel terms for the still newer universities, have diminished their usefulness. The designation 'civic' is neater and less loaded in meaning; it is also the term sanctioned by the usage of the UGC and the Robbins Committee. But we must be clear about what the word 'civic' does and does not mean. It means nothing more than that they all have their seat in a large town. It does not mean that the university, or the college which preceded it, was inaugurated or directly sponsored as a civic activity by the town, though that happens to be partly true, for example, of Liverpool; nor does it imply that financial help was immediately forthcoming from the rates to launch or even support the institution: the college at Manchester did not have a penny from the city until it had been in existence for forty years; nor does it mean that the university at the present time is of mainly local interest, drawing its students from a limited area: all of them have grown to be institutions of national significance with a student population coming from all parts of the kingdom and from overseas; and, above all, the term does not indicate that, even though the municipality may have a small minority of representatives on the governing bodies, the town controls the policy or the operations of the university in any way.

The university colleges: background

The civic universities all had their origin in what are conveniently referred to as 'university colleges': most of them indeed at one time or another had that designation as part of their title. These university colleges—a type of institution which has no close parallel elsewhere—were established sporadically and in a wide variety of ways in the second half of the nineteenth century and the first half of the twentieth. Some of them from the outset, and all of them in the course of time, provided teaching and engaged in research at a university level; but they did not have the right to award their own degrees, and those of their students who aimed at graduation followed the syllabuses and took the examinations for the external degree of London. What a contrast this is to the good fortune of the new universities founded since 1945, which from their inception were given the right to determine their own curriculum and to award their own degrees. Unlike Keele, Sussex, East Anglia, York, Essex, Lancaster, Kent, and Warwick, the university colleges had to serve a long, tedious, and often exasperating apprenticeship before they achieved independence. One important result of the broadly similar kind of conditions in which the civic universities evolved from embryonic university colleges is that all twelve bear a clear family likeness to one another: they have the same kind of constitution as defined in their charters and statutes; their procedures for internal government differ only in details; they conduct their academic and financial affairs in the same kind of way; and their entrance requirements and the structure of their courses of study for degrees are strikingly similar.

In a broad sense the university colleges were a somewhat belated response to the needs created by the industrial revolution. Expanding industry had come to depend more and more on a supply of people who possessed a wider range and a different kind of knowledge from that which had sufficed for a craft-based economy; and at the higher levels of education and training, it was the university colleges which eventually began to satisfy the ever growing needs. It would be misleading, however, to regard the foundation of these colleges as part of a concerted 'university college movement': the circumstances which led to the establishment of the individual institutions were too various and too haphazard to be so described, and the details of their separate histories show how uncertain some of them were at the beginning about their ultimate aims and purposes. Nor would it be right to think of the university colleges as being devoted solely to scientific and technical training. The motivations of those involved in their foundation were multifarious and complex. Hard-headed industrialists found themselves discussing with clergymen, doctors, and lawyers not only how provision was to be made for scientific and technical instruction but the more fundamental question of whether a place should be found in their emerging plans for the classics, history, literature, and philosophy. There was almost always a vision beyond what was of immediate utility, and in many instances specific provision was made right at the beginning for the arts and the learned professions.

Furthermore, the early history of these colleges has not only to be seen against the background of the practical needs of contemporary society, but interpreted also as a more general outcome of the intellectual vigour and enterprise of the provinces in the century or so preceding their foundation. It is in this connexion that some brief mention must be made of a few of the most important manifestations of a growing and widespread concern for education: the dissenting academies, the mechanics institutes, the medical schools, the cultural societies of many kinds, and (for the period from 1870 onwards) the University Extension movement.

The *dissenting academies* were an outcome of the 1662 Act of Uniformity which deprived a number of Oxford and Cambridge tutors of their college fellowships and many clergymen of their church livings. Some of these men set up academies of their own. One such, which was opened by Charles Morton at Newington Green in 1675, had Daniel Defoe and Samuel Wesley among its pupils; and the Attercliffe Academy, opened in Sheffield in 1688, had a great reputation in the north. Well over a hundred of these academies sprang up in various parts of the country: from Dartmouth, Taunton, and Exeter in the south, to Kendal and Whitehaven in the north; from Ipswich in the east to Bristol in the west. Their courses, which included English and history and some experimental science, covered as much as five years of study, and they provided for the mercantile classes and for some of the nobility a preferable alternative to the 'debauchery' of Oxford and Cambridge. They often enlisted the services of outstanding teachers, such as Joseph Priestley, who spent some years at Warrington, 'the Athens of the North'. Many of their pupils, amongst whom may be mentioned Thomas Secker, Archbishop of Canterbury, and Nicholas Saunderson, professor of mathematics at Cambridge, achieved positions of eminence. The academies began to decline, however, after 1800, through lack of endowments and a growing sectarianism within themselves; but they had exerted a great and permanent influence on a national scale, and many of the men whose names were prominent in the founding of the earlier university colleges had been pupils in them.

The *mechanics institutes* did not aim as high as the academies, being intended, at any rate in the first instance, to provide useful and practical instruction for artisans in evening classes. It may now seem a lowly aim. Yet one of the earliest, founded in London in 1824 under the inspiration of George Birkbeck, eventually became Birkbeck College and a constituent of the University of London; and the institute in Manchester developed into the College of Science and Technology. Other noteworthy institutes were set up in Sheffield, Leeds, Bradford, York, Wakefield, Newcastle, Leicester, and Nottingham; and by 1850 there were no fewer than 113 such institutes banded together in the Yorkshire Union alone. Throughout the country, by stimulating and doing much to satisfy a desire for knowledge and enlightenment, they rendered an invaluable service.

In relation to the rise of the university colleges, the *medical schools* in large cities were clearly of more immediate significance. The Apothecaries Act of 1815 had introduced some sort of order into the training and licensing of medical students; and the physicians and surgeons attached to the large charitable hospitals, which were founded in many towns during the second half of the eighteenth century, took in hand the task of organizing instruction in the hospitals for apprentice doctors. In many instances, it was men who were active in running these medical schools who took a leading part in crystallizing ideas which led to the foundation of a university college; and sooner or later, though not always without some heart-burning and hesitation, the medical school itself became affiliated to or incorporated in the new institution as its faculty of medicine.

Somewhat more generalized, but scarcely less potent in their influence, were the various *Literary and Philosophical Societies and Institutions* which grew up, notably in Manchester, Sheffield, Leeds, Liverpool, Bristol, Birmingham, and Newcastle, in the second half of the eighteenth century. Their membership in the main was middle-class, consisting of professional and business men, ministers of religion, and manufacturers, with an interest in culture. Serious in their aims, they provided single lectures and longer courses in literary, historical, and scientific subjects, and in some instances appointed part-time 'professors' of their own. They also collected learned libraries and even provided the nucleus of a museum. They had as their allies the more specialized historical, archaeological, and statistical societies; and in a loose sort of way they were encouraged by the Royal Society of Arts (founded in 1754) and by the activities of the British Association, which held its first meeting at York in 1831. The strange thing is that, although they had locally an influential membership and showed goodwill towards schemes for the establishing of a more permanent organization than their own, not a single one of them can be regarded as the real or putative parent of a university college.

More direct in its impact on the foundation of the later group of university colleges was the *University Extension* movement which was inspired by the missionary zeal of James Stuart, a young mathematical Fellow of Trinity College, Cambridge. He had the idea of 'a sort of peripatetic university of professors which would circulate in the big towns', and hoped that by this means permanent university establishments in the provinces might be made possible. After a successful course of lectures on gravitation which he gave in 1867 to audiences composed mainly of schoolmistresses in Leeds, Liverpool, Sheffield, and Manchester, he rallied support for a bolder plan, and by 1873 had induced the University of Cambridge to organize courses in English literature, political economy, and mechanics in Nottingham, Leicester, and Derby. By 1875 more than one hundred courses were being given by a group of lecturers under the Cambridge auspices. In 1876 London began to organize extension lectures of its own, and Oxford followed in 1878. It would be difficult to over-estimate the seminal importance of this movement. It had a direct and unmistakable connexion with the establishment of the university colleges in Sheffield, Nottingham, and Reading; it was in the front line in the battle for better education for women; and the provision which all universities now make for adult education through their departments of extra-mural studies is essentially a continuation of the work James Stuart began.

The university colleges: early difficulties

Such then is the general background. To unravel completely the tangled skein which is the collective and individual history of the university colleges is not within the scope of this book; but there are some dominant threads which it is necessary to define. It is evident that though a specific date can be given for the formal establishment of a college, the first steps towards that foundation were hesitant and tentative. Adumbrations of a 'university' or 'college' can generally be traced back many, many years before effective action was taken. Again and again we find that the enthusiastic president of a local cultural society or a distinguished visitor to a Literary and Philosophical institute would try to inspire local sentiment in the direction of founding a 'college' and even enunciate a 'plan for a university'. Memories of earlier proposals, such as the petition for a university presented to the Long Parliament by Manchester in 1640, would from time to time be recalled. More pertinent were the contrasts drawn between the lack of universities in England and the number of universities in Germany or the USA. In the main such seeds lay dormant. Sometimes, too, there was an institution actually in existence, such as Queen's College in Birmingham, which, had it possessed more vigour or found more support, could have been converted into the kind of college envisaged. But nothing tangible was achieved until some individual or some small group of determined people took the matter in hand.

Nor was there in existence any effective means whereby the various efforts leading to the foundation of the colleges in the different centres could possibly be co-ordinated. Undoubtedly the example of Owens College in Manchester was a powerful stimulus amongst interested circles in Leeds, Bristol, Sheffield,

Birmingham, and Liverpool; and the colleges established after 1900 could not fail to take the nineteenth-century colleges as their model. But all of them were established entirely by local effort and they got no help or encouragement from the government in their early years or even for long afterwards. It was local needs also that they set out to meet. Their prospective students were the young people of the immediate area; and except at Reading, residential accommodation formed no part of the original concept. From time to time these colleges did indeed combine to make approaches to the government for aid; but otherwise each of them worked out its academic and financial salvation as best it could.

The colleges did not have even a legal basis common to all. The colleges at Manchester, Sheffield, and Birmingham were first established under a trust deed executed by the founding benefactor; Liverpool was proudly launched with a royal charter and Southampton under a scheme of the Board of Education; the others were incorporated by a memorandum of association under the regulations of the Board of Trade. Years after its founding Owens College was reconstituted by an Act of Parliament, and Sheffield, Nottingham, and Leicester obtained royal charters as university colleges before becoming full universities.

At this present time, when large sums of money are voted by Parliament for capital and recurrent expenditure in support of the universities, and when students are pressing for admittance in their thousands, it is difficult to appreciate the troubles which beset the infant colleges. They began their work with the merest handful of professors and lecturers, and for years the senate or academic board could have been easily accommodated in a moderately sized drawing-room. Whatever the first expectations may have been, students did not flock to enter the new portals of learning, and in many colleges even the small number of students fluctuated up and down in a disconcerting way. Not all the students, by any means, came to read for a degree, and much comparatively elementary work had to be undertaken by the teaching staff, often enough in evening classes to meet the convenience of those who were arning a livelihood during the daytime. Indeed, until the 1902 Education Act empowered LEAs to establish and maintain secondary schools, the flow of students fit to embark on courses of real university standard was necessarily rather meagre.

Finance was a perpetual anxiety. The initial enthusiasms which greeted the foundation of a college wilted, donations and subscriptions proved hard to obtain or to renew, bequests were late in maturing, and the municipality often had qualms about entrusting more than a pittance from the rates to an institution over which it had no control. There were exceptions, of course, to this picture: the Wills family, for example, were notable benefactors to Bristol, the Boot family to Nottingham, and the Palmer family to Reading. But in the main the struggle for survival in the early years was grim. Four sources of revenue, however, came to hand to alleviate the situation. First, some courses given in the colleges were eligible for grants from the South Kensington Department of Science and Art which (under the aegis of the Education Department of the Privy Council) had been set up in 1856 to disburse the proceeds of the 1851 Exhibition by organizing science schools. Then, in 1889, the government was prevailed upon to allot £15,000 to be divided between the university colleges at Manchester, Leeds, Bristol, Sheffield, Birmingham, Liverpool, and Nottingham, together with Newcastle, Dundee, and University and King's Colleges in London. A condition of this grant was that the work of the colleges should be approved by visitors' (mostly heads of Oxford colleges) appointed by the government; and an important result of the continued application of this prudent principle was that inclusion on the 'list of institutions approved for purposes of grant' became the hallmark of academic standing.

Two other sources of central finance which helped the university colleges were 'whisky money' and payments for teacher-training. In 1890 part of the tax on spirits was diverted to the fostering of technical education, and in the distribution of the money some of the colleges had a share. It was in the same year 1890, that day colleges for the training of teachers were established by the Board of Education in close association with the

university colleges; and while the grants made to the student
enabled them to read for a degree concurrently with thei
professional training, the tuition fees paid to the colleges wer
a welcome addition to their income. Indeed, in some instances
this source of revenue rescued faculties of science and art
from near disaster.

The university colleges: pre-charter histories

Manchester. It was John Owens (1790–1846), a native of Flint
shire who had spent most of his life as a manufacturer an
merchant in Manchester, who brought to fruition ideas whic
had been in the air for more than half a century. In his wi
he left £96,000 to endow a college and appointed trustees t
guide its destinies. It was to provide 'the means of instructin
young persons of the male sex (and being of an age not les
than fourteen years) in such branches of learning and scienc
as are now or may be hereafter usually taught in the Englis
universities'. There was to be no test of religious opinions, an
preference was to be given to the children of parents residin
in or near Manchester. In March, 1851—a most noteworth
date in English education—Owens College opened its doo:
with three full-time and three part-time professors and sixty
two students. In formulating an academic policy the trustee
had been guided largely by what they had learned of th
curriculum in Scottish universities; it is not surprising there
fore that classics, literature, history, logic, and philosoph
found their place alongside mathematics and science. Until 187
control of the college was in the hands of the trustees: in th;
year they were superseded as the governing body, when th
college was formally incorporated by Act of Parliament an
the proscription against women was removed. Shortly afte:
wards the Royal School of Medicine (dating from 1824) wa
affiliated with it.

Leeds. For more than twenty years Owens College stoo
alone. Then in 1872 James Kitson, a Leeds engineer, stimulate
support for a scheme for setting up a college of science in th;
city; a constitution was adopted in 1874, and later in that yea
the Yorkshire College of Science began its work. In th

memorandum of association the object of the college was defined, somewhat differently from that of Owens, as follows: 'to promote the education of both sexes and in particular to provide instruction in such sciences and arts as are applicable or ancillary to the manufacturing, mining, engineering, and agricultural industries of the county of Yorkshire'. Public subscriptions were slow in coming; but encouragement was given by the Clothworkers Company of London to maintain a department of textile industries. Unlike Owens, the Leeds institution was at first wholly scientific, and though an arts section was added in 1877, it had for many years a hard struggle to survive. It was not until 1884 that the flourishing medical school (founded in 1831) was amalgamated with the College of Science.

Bristol, a city of culture as well as of commerce, was keenly alive to what was happening in the north. John Percival, Headmaster of Clifton School (founded in 1862) and later Bishop of Hereford, became the leader of a movement to found a college; in 1874 an influentially attended public meeting urged on the project; the medical school, which had been established in 1833 and by 1840 had itself envisaged Bristol as the 'seat of a medical university', supported the idea; and the Society of Merchant Venturers gave their blessing. There was enlightened help too from Oxford: Benjamin Jowett, Master of Balliol, offered the co-operation of his college and persuaded New College to do the same. By 1876, sufficient progress had been made for the college to be incorporated and begin its work with courses in history and literature as well as in science. The medical school became affiliated in 1879 and was fully incorporated in 1893.

Sheffield. The establishment of a college in Sheffield was due to the generosity of Mark Firth (1819–1880), a wealthy steel manufacturer. Impressed by the success of the Cambridge Extension courses in the city, Firth provided a site, a building, and an endowment for a college 'for the promotion of the moral, social and intellectual elevation of his fellow townsmen' and 'for the teaching and cultivation of any branch of learning'. With these broad and noble ideals the Firth College of Arts and Science was opened in 1879. By a royal charter it was amalgamated in 1897 with the Sheffield Technical School (founded in 1887 with the support of Firth College itself), and with the medical school (1828), under the title of University College.

Birmingham. Like Firth College, the Mason Science College in Birmingham owed its foundation to a great philanthropist. Sir Josiah Mason (1795–1881) had left school at the age of eight and, when he had become a prosperous industrialist, he used his wealth to found first an orphanage and then a college. He could have endowed the existing Queen's College (which from 1843 had embraced a medical school and departments of arts and theology) or the Midland Institute (which dated from 1854 and had an industrial department providing instruction in scientific subjects), but Mason preferred to devote £200,000 to founding a new institution. His college opened in 1880 and belied its seemingly exclusive title by appointing professors of classics and English in its first session. It was renamed Mason College in 1892, when the medical side of Queen's was merged with it, and it became Mason University College in 1898 by Act of Parliament. Queen's has become a wholly theological college, and the Midland Institute still exists with a flourishing school of music.

Liverpool. Civic pride gave birth to a university college in Liverpool. A town's meeting convened in 1878 by a group of leading citizens approved a scheme to found a college 'to provide such instruction in all branches of a liberal education as will enable residents in the town and neighbourhood to qualify for degrees in arts and science and other subjects'. The Royal Institution (founded in 1814), which sporadically had had its own 'professors', supported the scheme; the city provided a site and premises (a disused lunatic asylum) which could be adapted, and contributed liberally to an endowment fund. A royal charter of incorporation was granted in 1881 and the college opened in 1882. A medical school, established in 1834 and attached to the Royal Infirmary from 1844, was merged with the college in 1884.

Nottingham could be said to have stumbled almost unwittingly on a university college. A mechanics institute founded in 1837 had proved to be even more vigorous than usual, and not only provided classes in science which attracted financial help from the South Kensington Department of Science and Art, but served as a general focus for cultural activities. It was natural therefore that Nottingham in 1873 should ask Cambridge to send lecturers to the town under the University Extension scheme. These were so well attended that an anonymous donor offered £10,000 to provide a building for them. At this point the town council became associated with the project. It had already assumed responsibility for an artisans' free library and for the natural history museum of the mechanics institute. But both were in temporary premises. Why not have a new building for all three purposes? The donor of the £10,000 was agreeable, and the town found the balance of the funds required. By the time the 'University Extension building' was ready to be opened in 1881, a wider concept had emerged and the new institution was named University College. The committee of management, however, which was responsible for the college, was virtually under the control of the town council for many years; and it was not until 1903 that the college received a royal charter of incorporation.

Reading. One of the earliest centres for the Oxford University Extension movement was in the nearby town of Reading where a strong local association was formed. A number of senior members of Christ Church, Oxford, supported by Jowett of Balliol, worked for a more permanent organization. The outcome of these ideas was the setting up in 1892 of the University Extension College. The town council gave the use of two buildings on easy terms and transferred the management of its own School of Art and School of Science to the new institution. Classes were also provided for pupil teachers, and in 1893 a department of agriculture began its work. Formal incorporation came in 1898; and in 1902, when the institution was approved for receipt of a small government grant, it became officially known as University College.

Southampton. In 1850 H. R. Hartley, the son of a prosperous wine merchant, bequeathed £102,000 in his will to the Corporation of Southampton for 'the study and advancement of the sciences, natural history, astronomy, antiquities, and classical and oriental learning'. The will was disputed, and the Hartley Institute was not opened until 1862 with what remained of the money after the lawsuits. It comprised a museum, public library, art gallery, and lecture rooms. The institution failed to gain admittance in 1889 to the list of university colleges to share in government grants; but in 1902 it was successful in achieving the desired recognition; it was incorporated under a scheme of the Board of Education as Hartley University College, and its students began to read for London degrees.

Exeter has a complicated history. In 1865 the city erected a building, as a memorial to the Prince Consort, to house its art school (established in 1855), a county museum and a library. It was intended also to provide accommodation for courses in science and literature and for University Extension classes. In these early years some of the students were prepared for the South Kensington science and arts examinations, but nothing higher was aimed at. In 1893, when the classes had expanded, the city took the step of establishing the Exeter Technical and University Extension College, which from 1899 called itself the Royal Albert Memorial College; but it was not until 1901 that students began to present themselves for the external degrees of London. Slowly the institution began to aspire to the status which had been accorded to colleges in other cities; and finally in 1922, after several rebuffs, the institution was recognized for grant purposes and incorporated as the University College of the South West of England.

Leicester. The idea of a university college in Leicester can be traced as far back as 1880, and throughout all the subsequent discussions of the project a sense of rivalry with Nottingham can be felt to have been a motive force. In 1918 a group led by Dr. Astley V. Clarke convinced their fellow citizens that such a college could very fittingly be established as a war memorial; and in the next year T. F. Johnson paid £40,000 for the site and buildings of a former lunatic asylum and gave them to the town to house the college. This inauspicious birthplace has a parallel in the early history of the college at Liverpool. Donations from other citizens and help from the municipality enabled the college to begin work in 1921, and in that same year it was duly incorporated. It survived all the difficulties of the inter-war years and in 1945 was put on the UGC list for grant. In 1950 it received a royal charter as the University College of Leicester.

Hull, the last of the university colleges to be established before the second world war, came into being through the generosity of an individual benefactor. T. R. Ferens, a leading industrialist, donated £250,000 in 1925 specifically to endow a university college; the Corporation of Kingston-upon-Hull gave a site and a further £150,000 towards the cost of a building and equipment, and promised an annual grant. In 1927 the college was incorporated and began its work in 1928; but, like Leicester, it had to wait until 1945 before being recognized for grant purposes by the UGC.

Mention has already been made of the difficulties which the university colleges had to face. Yet not one of those which were established came to disaster, and for this there are two important reasons. In the first place, however indifferent the general public might be, there was always associated with the college a group of people who had its welfare at heart and were quite determined that it should *not* fail. They might be the trustees appointed under the founder's deed of settlement (as at Manchester, Sheffield, and Birmingham), or members of the college court and council appointed in accordance with the memorandum of association. Through thick and thin, these lay people worked for the college, served on committees, kept interest alive, gave and solicited donations, and discussed with the academic staff what needs had priority, and how those needs could best be met. Some of them had themselves been at Oxford or Cambridge and knew something of what was best in the university ideal. Others, it is true, were inclined at first to look on the academic staff as employees who had no right to a share in the formulation of policy; but they too came to see that if the college was to succeed, the court, council, and staff must be partners in a common enterprise. All these men have as their memorial the civic universities they helped to found.

The other factor which ensured the success of the colleges was the quality and devotion of the professors and lecturers who threw in their lot with these new institutions. Oxford and Cambridge men for the most part, they did not shrink from the prospect of teaching in grimy cities and in ungracious or repulsive buildings; nor did they shirk the drudgery of giving elementary instruction when it was needed. Dedicated to learning, scholars and scientists of repute, they had an unshakable faith not only that in the course of time the college as such would flourish, but that from it a full university would one day arise.

From college to university

As Owens College developed in stature after twenty years of trials and disappointments, a group of influential and distinguished professors began to urge with increasing insistence in the 1870s that the college should be elevated to full university status. The institution now had a life and character of its own, and research, alongside of teaching, was regarded as the vitalizing spirit of the place. But the need to prepare students for the London external degree was in every way irksome; and particularly galling was the fact that those who did the teaching had no say in the drawing up of the syllabuses or share in the examining. In 1877 the college authorities petitioned the Privy Council for the grant of a charter as an autonomous university. This proposal roused short-sighted opposition in Leeds, where the Yorkshire college was struggling to its feet, and in Liverpool, where already a movement was gaining strength for the setting up of a college: a fully chartered university in Manchester, it was thought, would put all other plans in jeopardy. No less than sixteen municipalities and scientific societies forwarded a counter-petition to the Privy Council.

After much negotiation another solution was suggested, and Manchester and Leeds agreed to present identical petitions for a federal university with its seat in Manchester: Owens College was to be its first constituent, and in due course other colleges might be incorporated within the federation. Thus in 1880 the Victoria University was established. It happened, however, that it was the new college in Liverpool (founded in 1881) which first satisfied the conditions for joining the federal university. This was in 1884. Leeds, which had less financial support from its locality and was still thought to be deficient on the arts side, had to wait until 1887. Sheffield was never admitted to the Victoria University. Its application in 1895 was refused because Firth College was not yet amalgamated with the technical college and the medical school; and its application in 1897 was so discourteously treated that its rejection was first made known through the press.

For a time the three constituents of the federal university rejoiced in their freedom from the London examinations; but internal dissatisfactions gradually became apparent and with them a desire for freedom from each other. All meetings of the university court were held in Manchester, as were meetings of examiners and the graduation ceremonies; there also had to be some common agreement about syllabuses and curricula. As the constituent colleges grew in size and prestige, friction increased. At this juncture Mason College in Birmingham rejected the idea which some there had advocated of a federal structure with Bristol and Nottingham; and under the dynamic drive of Joseph Chamberlain, the college applied for, and in 1900 obtained, its charter as an independent university. The pressure for independence already strong in Liverpool now became irresistible. In 1901, with the support of Manchester, Liverpool applied for its own charter; and, despite the firm opposition and counter-petition of Leeds, the charter was granted in 1903. It had, however, been indicated to Leeds that a petition for a charter of its own would be favourably considered, and in 1904 it too was given its charter. From this time onwards, the title of Victoria University was left in the sole possession of Manchester. It appears that in 1901 Sheffield would have been willing to consider a federal university for Yorkshire, even if its seat were in Leeds; but it was not willing that Leeds should alone be the University of Yorkshire. Honour, however, was now satisfied and ruffled feeling soothed

by the granting of a charter to Sheffield in 1905. The aspira-
tions of Bristol for full status as a university were fulfilled when
it received its charter in 1909.

Thus within the space of a single decade six separate universities had come into existence. The other four university
colleges already established (Nottingham, Reading, Southampton, and Exeter) had longer to wait. Their student numbers were small, their finances were weak; local interest in
some places was fitful; and cautious soundings in high quarters
about possible petitions for charters were coolly received. Had
not the country enough universities already? 'Standards must
be maintained.' Indeed, with the exception of Reading, which
obtained a charter in 1926, none of these colleges—nor either
of the two founded in the inter-war years (Leicester and Hull)
—was granted a charter until after the second world war. Then
the number of students applying for admission to universities
rapidly increased, and the provision of much greater financial
support for universities from central funds became government policy. The university colleges clearly could not be left
without the resources they required for full development; and
it was only as autonomous universities, entirely free to fashion
their own curricula and award their own degrees, that they
could achieve what was now expected of them. Nottingham
received its charter in 1948, Southampton in 1952, Hull in
1954, Exeter in 1955, and Leicester in 1957.

The newer universities

Keele. Even before the old chapter was neatly closed, a new
one opened with the foundation by royal charter in 1949 of a
quite different type of institution at Keele, near Newcastle-
under-Lyme, under the name of the University College of
North Staffordshire. Its location was an estate of 640 acres on
the fringe of a populous area which had no university institution near at hand, but which had long been a centre for the
University Extension movement. Its most energetic promoter
and its first Principal was Lord Lindsay, formerly Master of
Balliol. A number of local municipalities contributed funds,
but the major sustenance came from the UGC.

Its educational mainspring was a desire to break away from the traditional and over-specialized curriculum to which the other universities seemed bound, and in particular to bridge the gap between the arts and the sciences. As an essential part of a four-year undergraduate course, it fashioned a tripartite 'foundation year' common to all students, in which the pure sciences, the social sciences, and arts subjects were all studied. More will be said about this in Chapter II. The traditional faculties were replaced by boards of studies; and tutorial work cut across the boundaries of 'departments'. Constitutionally, its most novel feature was that, though not a university in name, it awarded its own degree of B.A., the standard of which was guaranteed by the sponsorship of the universities of Oxford, Manchester, and Birmingham. Furthermore, although near a large conurbation from which day-students might have been drawn, it was planned from the outset to be entirely residential for staff and students alike.

This wholly new venture roused the widest interest both at home and abroad. Some universities looked askance at this upstart and were annoyed that the UGC had barely consulted them before giving its approval. But there was no mistaking the fact that Keele was breaking loose from shackles, and its example has had a marked influence on the other universities which have been founded since. In 1962 it obtained a charter as the University of Keele and now awards higher degrees as well as its B.A. It remains, however, one of the smaller universities and is not planning for as rapid an expansion as most of its juniors.

There was little that was haphazard about the foundation of the seven other new universities; for they were deliberately established as part of a national policy to meet a growing and foreseeably insistent demand for university places. The universities and colleges existing in 1945 had had to cope immediately after the war with an influx of students returning from the armed forces, some to resume interrupted courses, others to take advantage of special educational grants. By 1952 most of these students had completed their studies; but pressure on the universities continued from other causes. The size of sixth forms in schools had shown a marked and steady growth (sometimes called the 'trend'), and a much greater number of school pupils were qualified to enter universities and desired to do so. The country was alive to university education at last. The possibility of obtaining a university education was made easy by the increase in the number and value of awards from public funds, both local and national.

In addition, it was foreseen that by 1961 the universities would be under still greater pressure as a result of the increase in the number of births in the last years of the war and up to 1947; the schools had had to handle this 'bulge' and, as pupils reached the sixth form, applications for entry to universities would become a serious problem. Apart from dealing with the ex-service students, the universities had already achieved by 1955 an expansion of numbers recommended by the 1946 Barlow Report on scientific manpower. How much more could they do? Furthermore, the proportion of students remaining in universities for postgraduate work was rising. It became evident that by the late 1960s and early 1970s the existing universities, however willing to help they might be, could not have enough places to match the demand: how, for example, alongside the other problems of planning and organizing a further expansion, could land be found for buildings in congested cities where housing was a clamant need?

At this stage the UGC tackled the problem. In 1946 (except for Keele) they had been against the foundation of more universities; but by 1955 the prospect was different. Local initiative and resources were now quite incapable of launching a new university; that was obvious from the fact that for existing universities 70 per cent. of annual recurrent expenditure and 90 per cent. of capital expenditure were being provided from government sources. It was only at government level that new universities could be started. What principles then should be applied in deciding upon new institutions?

First, two-thirds of the additional places in universities as a whole must be in pure and applied science, and the remainder in arts and social studies; and to this balance any new university must eventually contribute. Secondly, while the cost of acquiring sites in the centre of towns and cities would be too high, the need to find lodgings for students (until in due course residences could be provided), and the need to ensure that the staff was not cut off from good libraries and civilized amenities, could be met only by reasonable proximity to a well-established and vigorous community, with which a new institution could forge a mutually beneficial relationship. Thirdly, to plan with an ultimate target of anything less than 3,000 students would be uneconomic; and for such numbers an unencumbered site of at least 200 acres would be required. In the fourth place, there must also be evidence of local enthusiasm which would welcome the idea of having a university nearby, would provide some measure of financial support, participate in the running of the university by service on its council and its committees, and assist by putting industrial and other facilities at the disposal of the university when need arose. Finally, the new institutions ought to be free to experiment with the curriculum, as Keele had been, and not be tied to any existing kind of degree structure; and they might wish also to adopt a constitutional pattern different from that of Oxford and Cambridge or the civic universities. From this it followed that any new institutions should not be university colleges but autonomous universities established by royal charter and empowered to award their own degrees.

There certainly was no lack of local enthusiasm in various parts of the country. To be the seat of a university was a symbol of status. In Brighton, York, and Norwich proposals for a university college (at least) had been mooted for many years and were revived after the war; these three were at the head of the queue. Within a short space enquiries reached the UGC from twenty other places in England and eight in Scotland; but seven was the number of new universities the UGC was prepared to recommend to the government, and a selection had to be made. Between 1957 and 1961 official encouragement to formulate definitive plans was given to Brighton, York, Norwich, Colchester, Canterbury, Lancaster, and Coventry. They were all places which the UGC was satisfied would meet the criteria they had in mind as regards local financial support, suitable sites, and accommodation for students. The University of Sussex (at Brighton) was granted its charter in 1961; York followed in 1963, East Anglia (at Norwich) and Lancaster in 1964, Essex (at Colchester), Kent (at Canterbury), and Warwick (at Coventry) in 1965. In most cases the first students were admitted a year earlier than the charter.

The procedure adopted in founding these new universities is of sufficient general interest to be recorded. First of all, local ambitions expressed themselves through a 'promotion committee', generally sponsored officially by the municipality. This committee mobilized financial support in its area and elsewhere, arranged for a site, and drew up a case for submission to the UGC. When a project was approved, an 'academic planning board', consisting in the main of people of high academic standing in other universities, was set up in the closest consultation with the UGC. It was the function of this board to select and recommend for appointment a vice-chancellor, the first key members of the academic staff, and the chief administrative officers, and to prepare a draft for a charter and statutes. These tasks involved two or three years of hard work and thought. The new charters all contain provision for an academic advisory board, not wholly identical with the transient planning board, to consult with the new university in its early years—but not to dictate to it—in the matters of general policy, curriculum, and standards of degrees. This device is a refinement of the sponsorship which watched over the early years of Keele. At the end of ten years, or possibly earlier, these advisory boards will cease to function.

In later chapters more will be said about the educational and constitutional innovations at these new universities. Here there are two things of importance to be noted. In the first place, they all have from their inception a clear idea of the amount and rate of expansion for which they are willing to plan; and they have as reasonable an assurance as any government can give that, even if not pampered by the UGC to the detriment of other universities, they will not be frustrated from achieving their aims through desperate lack of money. How different a

picture is this from the hand to mouth progress of the university colleges! The second point is that, just as the university
colleges were fortunate in attracting outstanding persons to
join their staff and help the ventures along, so these newer
universities have been able to enlist the help of some of the
most forward-looking people from the staffs of other universities to lay their academic foundations.

The strain which this loss of staff put on the existing universities has not been serious; but the benefit to the younger
foundations is immeasurable. Here there was a challenge to
participate in the modelling of a new university from its earliest
beginnings; the key men brought with them not only a training
and a belief in the best of the traditional, but a willingness and
an eagerness to re-think the purposes and ideals of a university
in a rapidly changing world of science and technology. They
started their work with nothing more than a spacious estate
and an old mansion generously donated by a local authority;
they had to take far-reaching decisions on their broad academic
policy and strategy, to detail a programme for the physical
development of the site, and plan academic and residential
accommodation; and, amid the bustle and noise of building
contractors, they selected and admitted their first groups of
students.

The Robbins expansion and the CATs

From 1955 onwards the UGC paid much attention to forecasting
and planning for increased numbers of places in universities
in future years; in 1962 the government had accepted the
UGC's advice that the targets for the existing universities (including the seven new ones that were being founded) should
be 150,000 by 1966–7 and 170,000 by 1973–4, though one
estimate had been as high as 200,000 for 1973–4. These figures
were based partly on the evidence of demand for places, partly
on the rate at which universities had actually been expanding in
recent years, and partly on forecasts of the national need for
graduates in various fields.

The Robbins Report, published in 1963, surveyed the whole

field of higher education and made a number of recommendations about universities in particular which have changed the
entire picture. The report was based on two crucial doctrines.
The first was that 'courses of higher education should be
available for all those who are qualified by ability and attainment to pursue them and wish to do so'. This principle must
assume that the individual student will not be debarred by
lack of money from pursuing the course of study for which he
is acceptable, and that in consequence the country can in some
way afford to finance the students themselves and maintain the
institutions in which they are to be enrolled; and a further
assumption is that whatever the number of such students may
be, the national need for graduates is such that they can be
found suitable work on which their talents and training can
properly be used. How far these assumptions are valid only
time can show; but it is worth noting that they are assumptions
and not proven facts. The second doctrine was the 'principle
of equal academic awards for equal performance'. In the harsh
world of reality, which knows that 'parity of esteem' is a
hollow mockery, this could only mean that work of degree
standard, wherever and however it is achieved, should be
accorded a degree. The logical outcome of this has been the
setting up by royal charter in 1964 of the National Council
for Academic Awards, of which more will be said later.

In terms of numbers the report calculated that by 1967-8
a total of 328,000 full-time places would be needed in higher
education as a whole, and of this number 197,000 students
should be in institutions of university status; by 1973-4, out
of a total of 392,000 for all higher education, 218,000 should
be the number in universities; and for 1980 the corresponding
figures were tentatively put at 560,000 and 350,000. These
figures were appreciably in advance of anything previously
contemplated; but in face of the statistical evidence on which
they were calculated, the government accepted them as a basis
for planning up to 1973-4. Later official estimates show that
Robbins was probably not bold enough. In some university
circles so rapid an increase from the 120,000 students they had
in 1962-3 was viewed with mingled incredulity and alarm,

but the phrase 'university institution' was taking on a different connotation.

To implement such a plan of expansion the main recommendations of the report were: that many of the existing universities should increase their student numbers to 8,000 or 10,000; that Colleges of Advanced Technology (CATs) should in general be given status as technological universities, derive their financial support through the UGC, and be empowered to award first and higher degrees; that six additional new universities should be founded, of which one at least should be in Scotland; and that a small number of Special Institutions for Scientific Education and Research (acronymically 'sisters') should be developed with university status along the lines of the great technological institutes of America, Holland, and Switzerland. Of these four major proposals the last two were rejected by the government, which announced in 1965 that, apart from a new university at Stirling in Scotland and a primarily postgraduate technological university in the north-east of England on Teeside, no entirely new university institution would be founded within the following ten years.

The existing universities, knowing from experience what are the difficulties of planning and building new academic and student accommodation, and despite their serious anxieties about securing additional staff of adequate calibre, faced the responsibilities placed upon them, if not gladly, at least with resignation. They are now expanding as quickly as the irritatingly intermittent flow of government finance for buildings permits. Nor were they unduly sensitive about what they regarded as their prerogative to award degrees: they had some years previously agreed that the work done in CATs for the Diploma in Technology (Dip.Tech.), awarded by the then National Council for Technological Awards, was academically equivalent to a good honours degree, and as such was acceptable as evidence justifying admission to a postgraduate course in a university. The proposal to raise the CATs to university status did nothing to ruffle the waters of academic composure.

Before 1956 no one had heard of CATs. In that year, under a Ministry of Education reorganization scheme, institutions pro-

vided and maintained by LEAs for full- and part-time furthe
and higher technical education were grouped as local, area
regional, and advanced colleges. In this last group, the CAT:
there were ten institutions selected to concentrate on full-tim
courses of an advanced level, including the preparation o
students for the Dip.Tech. and the external London degree:
and to develop their research sides. Four of them are in Londo
and the home counties: Battersea, Brunel (formerly Acton)
Chelsea and Northampton; the other six are in Birmingham
Bradford, Bristol, Cardiff, Loughborough, and Salford. In 196
it was thought desirable to divorce these ten colleges from the
control and responsibility of LEAs, to give them under a trus
deed an independent governing body on which LEAs, univer
sities, and industry were represented, and to finance them by
direct grants from the Ministry.

Since their designation in 1956 these colleges have shown
remarkable energy and initiative. The number of full-time
students in attendance reached 10,000 in 1962, 14,000 in 1964
and 16,000 in 1965. By 1964 some 4,000 of their students had
gained the Dip.Tech. Their research activities were assiduously
fostered; sites were secured for new buildings; halls of resi
dence were erected. Educationally their great contribution ha
been the development, partly on American patterns, of sand
wich courses which enable students to alternate periods of
practical experience in industry with periods spent in college
on academic studies. For such an integrated training and
education, close relations with industry have been established
Furthermore, many of the colleges, even before their partia
emancipation in 1962, had begun to provide courses in econom
ics, sociology, management, and administration, without which
they felt, a purely technological training would be incomplete
and of much less value to the students and the community.

From April, 1965, all these colleges were placed on the
UGC grant list, which ensures that their needs will be con
sidered (and not ungenerously) in relation to those of other
universities. Academic salaries have been brought into line
with those in universities, so that staff recruitment will not be
hampered by financial disparities; an academic advisory com-

mittee has been set up for each college to help in the formulation of policy, the making of key appointments, and the draft-
ing of a charter; and many posts of professorial status and title
have already been filled, mainly by the redesignation of heads of
departments; and it is expected that by the end of 1966 almost
all the CATs will have been granted a charter.

Most of them are bashfully eschewing the word 'technological' in their title, and some are moving from their present sites.
Battersea proposes to become the University of Surrey, with
its seat at Guildford, and Brunel University will have its seat
in Uxbridge. The Birmingham college becomes the University
of Aston in Birmingham, and Bradford the University of
Bradford. The Bristol college moves to Bath with the title of
the University of Bath. Loughborough (a long-established
college which was once thought of as a constituent of a
federal university with the university colleges at Leicester and
Nottingham) becomes the Loughborough University of
Technology; and Salford becomes the University of Salford.
The Northampton CAT (in Clerkenwell) becomes the City
University; but Chelsea will be federated in some way with
London, as Cardiff will with Wales.

The Manchester College of Science and Technology,
founded by the municipality in 1902, became closely identified
in 1905 with the faculty of technology in the University of
Manchester and the advanced students of the college took the
degrees of the university in engineering. During the inter-war
years the college was separately recognized by the UGC for
inclusion in its list of grant-aided institutions. The Robbins
Committee grouped it with the Royal Technical College at
Glasgow and Imperial College in the University of London for
special development. But whereas the Glasgow college has
become the University of Strathclyde, the one in Manchester
is for the time being satisfied with a change of its name to the
University of Manchester Institute of Science and Technology.

Wales

One of the heroes of Welsh history, Owain Glyndwr, in 1406
(five years before the founding of St. Andrews) proposed the

establishment of two universities to serve North and South Wales, as one of the terms of an alliance with Charles VI of France. But Wales had to wait nearly five hundred years. The first practical step was the opportunist purchase in 1867, by a group of enthusiasts, of a bankrupt hotel on the sea-front at Aberystwyth. This was to be the seat of a college; yet by the time it opened in 1872 to receive its first handful of students, three-quarters of the purchase price had still to be found; and the story of how Sir Hugh Owen, the leader of the movement, and his friends travelled up and down Wales addressing meetings and collecting money, much of it in the sixpences contributed by miners and quarrymen, is one of the minor epics of educational endeavour. The college struggled on, the government gave a small grant from 1882, and a royal charter was granted to the college in 1889. Aberystwyth, however, was not easily accessible from other parts of Wales, and not surprisingly both North and South Wales determined that they should have colleges of their own. One such college opened in Cardiff in 1883, another in Bangor in 1884, and both received royal charters in 1884. All three colleges prepared their students for the external degrees of London until 1893, when they became federated in the University of Wales, with its central administrative headquarters in Cardiff. Under this arrangement the colleges retain their identity and handle their own finances; and the vice-chancellorship of the university is held in rotation by the principals of the colleges.

A royal commission in 1916-18 resulted in a new charter in 1920, which enlarged the freedom of individual colleges to arrange their own syllabuses and founded a fourth college at Swansea (which had been a contender with Cardiff in the 1880s for the first college in South Wales). A further supplemental charter in 1932 defined the position of the Welsh National School of Medicine at Cardiff as a school of the university. In the 1950s, as the number of students in the colleges grew, earlier talk of breaking up the federal structure and giving full university status to each of the colleges was revived; but in 1964 the court of the university, after considering two conflicting reports submitted by a commission it had set up in

1960, reaffirmed the principle of federation. There the matter stands: but the tale is perhaps not yet fully told.

Of all academic anomalies, *St. David's College* at Lampeter in mid-Wales, is one of the most bizarre. Founded in 1822—note the date—on the initiative of Thomas Burgess, Bishop of St. David's, to provide instruction and residential accommodation for theological students who were unable 'by reason of the expense to pursue their studies in the English universities', it received a royal charter in 1829. By a further charter in 1852 it was empowered to award the degree of B.D., while another charter of 1865 validated its degree of B.A. In 1896 the college abolished religious tests for students. Though always small in numbers, the college took pride in the fact that Oxford appointed external examiners and recognized the degrees. But until recently no links were forged between this Anglican foundation and the university of a predominantly nonconformist Wales. An application to be put on the UGC grant list in 1955 was unsuccessful; but in 1961 there was a more fortunate outcome under a ten-year scheme whereby the college at Cardiff (not the one at Aberystwyth, which is only twenty miles away) undertook the role of sponsor, providing help in the teaching and the drawing up of syllabuses. The growth of St. David's is to be limited in arts to 250 students and the degrees awarded will still be those of St. David's.

Ireland

It needs patience and a cool head to thread one's way through the ramifications of university history in Ireland. But one thing is clear: the pride of place is held by Trinity College, Dublin. Founded by a royal charter in 1592, it was intended to be the first constituent of a University of Dublin; but no other college was founded under the provisions of the charter, and 'T.C.D.' and the University of Dublin have remained for all practical purposes interchangeable terms. The wide and autocratic powers of control vested by the charter in the provost and the senior fellows of the college were abridged by Charles I, but largely restored by the Crown in 1911. For over 200 years Trinity was the only university in Ireland. In the roll of its graduates there appear the names of many of the outstanding figures in Irish scholarship, science, medicine, law, and politics. Situated in the very heart of the capital city, it has played a prominent part in Irish cultural life; and though an Anglican foundation, and for long associated inevitably with the English domination, it has survived all political upheavals. It now has three representatives in the Irish Senate, and more than a third of its annual revenue comes from grants made by the Republic of Ireland.

In 1845, which by one of the bitter ironies of history was the first year of the great Irish famine, the government in London established by royal charter three non-sectarian 'Queen's Colleges', at Belfast in the north, Cork in the south, and Galway in the west. They were to be part of a plan 'for extending university education in Ireland'; but the political considerations underlying the gesture are plain to see: Daniel O'Connell's agitation for repeal of the union with England was gaining strength, and Catholic opinion was hostile to Trinity College. The three colleges opened for students in 1849, and in 1850 they were linked together as the Queen's University of Ireland. The Catholic hierarchy, so far from being appeased, took the step of founding in 1851, in Dublin itself, the Catholic University of Ireland. This institution began its work in 1854 and had as its first Rector (from 1851 to 1859) John Henry Newman, the future Cardinal. The next move in this unhappy story came in 1879 when the Queen's University not only had its title changed to the Royal University of Ireland, but its functions were restricted to the control of the syllabuses and examinations for degrees; and since its degrees could now be taken externally, there was a serious drop in the number of students attending the three colleges. A few years later, in 1883, the Catholic University changed its name to University College, Dublin, and came under the administration of the Jesuit Fathers.

A more lasting arrangement was finally arrived at in 1908 as a result of the Irish Universities Act. The present National University of Ireland was then founded, with the two former Queen's Colleges at Cork and Galway and the renamed University College, Dublin, as its constituents; and the college at Belfast was given a separate charter as the independent Queen's University of Belfast with a constitution similar to that of an English civic university.

With the establishment of the Government of Northern Ireland in 1920, Queen's, Belfast, became even more closely identified with Ulster and since that year has derived a progressively increasing proportion of its revenue from that government. In 1945 the UGC was invited by the government of Northern Ireland to advise it on the financial needs of the university and has continued to do so from time to time. In 1965 the government of Northern Ireland, to the great disappointment of Londonderry, decided to establish a second university at Coleraine, to be a centre for the biological sciences, agriculture, and teacher-training; and to associate with it the small Magee University College in Londonderry which has hitherto had affiliations with both Queen's, and Trinity.

2
Universities at Work

Teaching and research

THESE ARE THE TWO COMPLEMENTARY ACTIVITIES to which most of the energies of a university in the modern world are directed. The balance between the giving of instruction and the advancement of knowledge has varied very greatly from age to age. In the mediaeval universities teaching almost entirely predominated; but part at least of the attraction exerted by these early centres of learning lay in the fact that many of those who taught in them were not only men of erudition in their own generation but were also pioneers in thought. In every century there were men in the universities who, in one way or another, added to the sum of knowledge and enlarged the range of scholarly and scientific speculation. A real consciousness, however, of the importance of original investigations and of deliberately organized effort, especially in the fields of science, is one of the main characteristics of university development in the nineteenth century. Nowadays, a university which neglected either teaching or large-scale research would not be considered to be justifying its title.

Within a university context there is no opposition between teaching and research: the two interact upon one another. Teaching that is confined merely to the handing on of what is known or deemed to be known, in the long run becomes pedantic and lifeless: that was notoriously the fate of mediaeval scholasticism. But when a teacher is himself engaged on work at the frontiers of knowledge and thought, the quality of all his teaching is subtly vivified. It is a common experience that when inquiring closely into a chosen topic, so far from narrowing his interests, a researcher not only finds himself picking up a surprising amount of miscellaneous information about his subject in general but gets his subject into a new and revealing perspective. The stimulating effect on teaching of this wider vision and more comprehensive grasp is something to which anyone who has been subjected to it can testify. On the other hand, an alert approach on the part of the teacher to the content and the validity of what he is teaching, no matter how well worn the theme or commonplace the subject, will often enough suggest the need for reconsideration or further inquiry and so lead on to research.

This brings us at once to what is the most important point about the nature of teaching and education at a university level. It must necessarily provide the student with a body of positive knowledge which enhances his store of learning and in part equips him for his career in later life. But it also has another and more notable attribute. It inculcates in the student an attitude of mind which regards the critical assessment of facts and values as more important than dogmas, and which holds that a grasp of underlying principles is more valuable than the accumulation of information or the acquisition of skills and techniques. A university expects that at the end of their courses its students will not merely be able to comprehend the extent and significance of what is already known within their own field, but will be receptive to what is new, eager to explore it, show the ability to cope with it, and—above all—be able to work confidently on their own. By entering a university a student has undertaken to accept a rigorous intellectual discipline and to be more than a passive receptacle for information, much of which in many subjects may be out of date within twenty years. To the limit of his capacity, he is trained to collect evidence for himself and form a balanced judgement about it. He fortifies his ability to think for himself; he refuses to accept orthodoxies simply because they are orthodox; and when he dissents, he does so on the basis not of prejudice but of reason. This is what good teaching achieves in a university.

The freshman entering a university, though full of adolescent enthusiasms, does not always realize what is in store for him. No one really believes that the 169,000 students in universities in 1966, or the 350,000 who may be there by 1980, are dedicated to knowledge for its own sake. Theirs is no disinterested pursuit of learning. Talk to most students and you will find that their reasons for seeking entry into a university are mixed and not always wholly clear to themselves. It is not that they are allergic to learning: undoubtedly, by reason of their natural talents and their earlier training, they are intellectually inclined; but their focus is often blurred. A student may have come partly because, for a young man or woman with some measure of mental ability and achievement, going to a university is now the conventional and desirable pattern of life; his headmaster, his parents, and his older friends have for years imbued him with the idea that the securing of a place in a university is almost a goal in itself; and he knows in a vague way that education in a university is somehow a good thing; but only the quite exceptional student has it firmly in mind at the outset that his own life may be dedicated to learning. If there is one common factor which brings students to a university it is the belief that when they have earned a degree they will have gone some long way towards fitting themselves for a career. Every medical student intends to become a physician or surgeon; every engineering student foresees a time when his livelihood and main occupation will be in engineering; most law students have a legal practice of some kind in mind; and even if, as a freshman, the arts student may not be so specific in his expectation, he is aware in a general way of the avenues which will be open to him in a variety of callings: schoolteaching, social work, the civil service, broadcasting, or the managerial side of commerce and industry. Every teacher in a university is fully and sympathetically aware of the strength of this vocational motivation which in part brings students to them. But their own critical approach to what they teach, and the ways in which they organize the presentation of their subjects, add perspective to that vocational element, open up wider horizons, and give to education in a university its distinctive lavour. In this sense students do indeed get more than they bargained for.

The scope of university studies

The curriculum of the mediaeval university was very closely related to the vocational needs of the times. Based on a preliminary training in the seven liberal arts and philosophy, the higher faculties of theology, law (canon and civil), and medicine had the manning of the learned professions in view. The charters and privileges granted by the Popes who confirmed the establishment of *universitates* were not given from any altruistic desire to encourage original thought: that might lead to heresy; they were given primarily to safeguard and improve the quality of the higher clergy. Temporal rulers, for their part, looked with favour on universities—when they did not misbehave—because it became evident that in them people were trained who were capable of discharging essential administrative and legal functions for the monarch and the state. It would be a mistake, however, to dismiss the mediaeval curriculum as lacking in breadth; in any case it was the higher faculties rather than the requirements for the degree of bachelor which were distinctively vocational. In the circumstances of the times, the curriculum taken as a whole covered the entire range of human knowledge; and the example of the scientifically minded Roger Bacon (1214–1294) at Oxford is sufficient proof that myopic concern with the minutiae of philosophical and theological disputation was not the whole story.

The scientific revolution of the sixteenth and seventeenth centuries, and the work of men like Galileo, Francis Bacon, and William Harvey, finally destroyed the edifice of scholastic philosophy and the Aristotelian concept of the universe. The broadening of the scope of university studies became inevitable; but formal recognition of the legitimacy of scientific studies was slow in coming. Mathematics and astronomy, which were traditional parts of the old curriculum, had always been kept alive: the Savile chair of geometry and astronomy was founded at Oxford in 1619, and the chair of mathematics which Newton later held was founded at Cambridge in 1663; botany, which had its special relevance for medicine and therapeutics, had a chair at Oxford from 1669; chemistry too had a chair there from 1683. In other scientific subjects, however, progress was desultory. Though an honours school in natural science was established in Oxford in 1850 and in Cambridge in 1851, and though many colleges in both universities provided instruction and small laboratories in branches of the natural sciences, the emphasis in both universities as a whole remained on classics philosophy, and mathematics.

It is perhaps not unfair to say that it was the university colleges in the large towns which made many of the sciences fully respectable as academic subjects. Professorships in physics, chemistry, and engineering were amongst their early appointments; and as newer subjects, such as biochemistry bacteriology, veterinary science, and agriculture emerged, it was the civic universities which were likely to be the first to establish separate chairs and departments. But at Cambridge the Cavendish laboratory for experimental physics was not established until 1871 and the corresponding Clarendon laboratory was opened in Oxford only in 1872. A chair of engineering science came belatedly at Oxford in 1907, an electrical engineering laboratory in 1910, and a chair of biochemistry in 1920. This kind of chronology, however, could be wildly misleading; for Oxford and Cambridge have come to be ranked amongst the foremost universities of the world in pure science and in many branches of applied science. A similar account would have to be given in regard to some arts subjects. In the older universities, English literature, modern languages, economics, and sociology, for example, were for an unduly long time not given serious attention or the professorial dignity they had achieved in the civic universities: they were treated as being dilettante. On the other hand, the university colleges, in their determination to avoid any suspicion of imposing religious or sectarian tests, at first turned a cold shoulder on theology, which had once been called 'the queen of the sciences'.

It would, of course, be uneconomic and indeed impracticable for every university to attempt to include every subject within its scope. The legitimate and reasonable requirements for (say) textile technology, Indian archaeology, oceanography, Celtic, or production engineering can best be met by concentration in a few properly equipped centres. Outside the hard core of mathematics, physics, chemistry, botany, zoology, geology, classics, English, French, German, history, geography, and economics, there are many subjects which are not available in all universities for a first degree. For example, there is no medical faculty at Reading, Southampton, Hull, or Leicester, and one is only now in process of formation at Nottingham; only twelve universities offer first degree courses in agriculture, eight in veterinary science, five in forestry; Chinese can be studied seriously only in five, Japanese only in three.

In the modern world there are two main reasons which lead to the inclusion of new subjects in the work of a university. The first is natural growth: as knowledge within an older subject expands, a process of fission takes place, and chemistry comes to be manageable only in its separate aspects of inorganic, organic, and physical; or some special area assumes a new significance, and colour chemistry acquires an identity of its own; Rutherford splits the atom, Chadwick discovers the neutron, and a consequential distinction arises between classical and particle physics; electrical engineering and physics hive off electronics and cybernetics; departments of drama are an offshoot of English literature. It is also at the boundaries between two disciplines that the growing points for new subjects are found: such are chemical engineering, genetics, psychiatry, biophysics, immunochemistry, materials science, and psycholinguistics. The refinement of equipment too can play its part, as in the cases of microbiology and computer science.

The second factor which brings new subjects within the fold is the willingness of universities to respond to new needs of society which they alone are in a position to meet satisfactorily. It is national requirements, quite as much as academic considerations, which have led since 1945 to the increase in the number of departments of Russian and the setting up of new departments of American, Latin-American, and Far-Eastern studies. Sometimes too there are outside pressures from professional bodies, which value the prestige and quality of a university degree and are eager for universities to participate in the training of new entrants to the professions: hence we now have degrees in accountancy, public administration, nursing (as a branch of sociology), estate management, and business studies. Two of the former CATs have already gone further and have accepted an endowment from an industrial organization for chairs in hotel and catering management and administration. Much heart-searching is occasioned in universities before proposals to include vocational newcomers are accepted. It is always argued, and not by the traditionalists alone, that they are trivial, wasteful of resources, and have no real place in a university. But in practice the problem is resolved by applying principles which are clear and unmistakable: any subject taught in a university must have a definite and substantial content of fundamental knowledge, must be within an area where further advances in knowledge are possible, and must not be predominantly a training in skills and techniques. Any serious departure from these principles, no matter how great the outside pressure or how tempting the financial inducements, diverts a university from its more important functions and fritters away its energies.

The balance of studies

The easiest approach to an appreciation of the existing balance of studies in universities will be by way of the following Table 1, which gives figures and percentages for the last pre-war session and for the latest session for which statistics are available. In this Table the category of arts subjects includes law, economics, and commerce as well as social studies; the 'others' consist of agriculture, forestry, and veterinary science. The numbers given for postgraduate students in 1963–4 exclude 3,801 graduates in arts and science who were taking a one-year course in teacher-training.

A number of interesting facts can be elicited from Table 1. As between 1938–9 and 1963–4, the changes in the percentages and in absolute numbers show a marked swing towards pure and applied science; these two categories taken together have increased from 25·9 to 41·7 per cent., and in numbers have more than quadrupled from 12,949 to 52,808. This trend is the result of several factors: the policy of the government to foster these subjects by liberal financial support, the readiness of the universities to co-operate, and the change of balance between arts and science in sixth forms in schools. Nevertheless some anxiety has been felt since 1962 because the universities have not been able to fill with properly qualified students all the

Table 1: Full-Time Students by Faculties

		1938–9		1963–4	
		Nos.	%	Nos.	%
A:	Total students:	50,002	100·0	126,445	100·0
	Arts & social studies	22,374	44·7	54,529	43·1
	Pure science	7,661	15·3	34,315	27·1
	Technology	5,288	10·6	18,493	14·6
	Medicine & dentistry	13,636	27·3	15,839	12·6
	Others	1,043	2·1	3,269	2·6
	Postgraduates included in the above total	3,094	6·2	18,754	14·9
B:	Postgraduates:	3,094	100·0	18,754	100·0
	Arts & social studies	1,175	38·0	6,494	34·6
	Pure science	1,268	41·0	6,882	36·7
	Technology	388	12·5	3,551	18·9
	Medicine & dentistry	198	6·4	1,359	7·2
	Others	65	2·1	468	2·6

Note:—In 1963–4 there were also 16,528 part-time students. Of these 1,351 were reading for a first degree, 766 for a first diploma; and 6,814 were doing advanced work. Half of these part-time students were in the University of London. Of those reading for a first degree or diploma, almost one half were in arts and social studies; of the advanced students, 44 per cent. were in arts and social studies and 36 per cent. in medicine.

places available in science and technology. It is a stubborn fact of life that many pupils do really prefer literature, history, languages, and geography to science—and still more to engineering, which they wrongly associate with oily hands. The arts group of subjects has in fact all but maintained its percentage, even though its more than twofold increase in numbers has been at a slower rate than that of science and technology. The increase in the number of medical and dental students, however, has been small—only 2,200 in twenty-five years—and the percentage has dropped from 27·3 to 12·6. Policy in high quarters has not been directed until recently to any substantial increase in the number of medical students, and a drive for more dental students did not begin until the mid-1950s.

A very noteworthy change has taken place since 1938–9 in the proportion of full-time students pursuing postgraduate courses and research. The percentage has risen from 6·2 to 14·9, and the numbers are six times as great. The distribution of postgraduates between the various disciplines has remained fairly stable, the most marked percentage increase being in technology. Of these postgraduate students, 7,271 come from overseas, divided almost equally between Commonwealth and foreign countries. Of home-born students who take a first degree, about 20 per cent. now proceed to postgraduate work (apart from teachers in training). The Robbins Committee recommended that this percentage should be increased to thirty by 1980.

Degrees and curricula

The culmination of an undergraduate's career in a university is the award of a first degree of 'bachelor'. In general, the title of the degree gives some indication of the kind of course which has been followed: bachelor of arts, of law, of science, of engineering, of architecture, of medicine and surgery, and so forth. Postgraduates are awarded the degree of 'master' in their own faculty or (at a more advanced level) of 'doctor in philosophy' (Ph.D.), a title which is common to all faculties. The higher doctorates, as D.Sc. or D.Litt., are awarded on the evidence of a body of published work contributing substantially to knowledge. Honorary masters' degrees and the higher doctorates may be conferred on persons distinguished in learning or in public life.

There are a few important divergencies, however, from the normal scheme. At Oxford and Cambridge the B.A. is the only first degree awarded: it covers arts, pure and applied science, theology, law, and the pre-clinical part of the medical course. The B.Sc., which is a first degree elsewhere, is a higher degree at Oxford but does not even exist at Cambridge. In the four older universities of Scotland the first degree in arts is the M.A. The word bachelor is also used at Oxford and Cambridge, and at other universities, for some higher degrees, such as B.Mus., B.Phil., B.Litt., LL.B. At Oxford and Cambridge the M.A. is not, as elsewhere, awarded on examination or for research, but it is taken by B.A.'s of several years' standing on payment of a fee.

Another term, 'diploma' is used for some first and for some higher qualifications which do not rank as a degree. As a first qualification, diplomas used to be awarded to students who took a full degree course, but who had not satisfied normal entrance requirements for matriculation; but it is now mostly awarded for a course which is of shorter duration than that for a first degree. As a higher qualification, a diploma is given for some specialized postgraduate courses, as in education, public health, tropical medicine, archive administration, anthropology, classical archaeology. In 1938–9, out of 50,002 full-time students 7,679 were reading for a first diploma; in 1963–4 the number was only 3,390 out of 126,445. In some subjects 'certificates' are awarded for courses less exacting than those for a diploma or degree.

First degrees. In the majority of universities in England and Wales, and in most subjects, the course of study leading to a first degree normally extends over three years; in arts 8 per cent. of students take courses which are longer, in science 14 per cent., and in technology 22 per cent.; the courses in medicine and dentistry, however, are planned on the basis of five or more usually six years. In Scotland the first degree is a four-year course. Many universities would prefer that all first degree courses in arts and pure science should occupy four years of study, on the ground that with the growth of knowledge it is difficult to bring students up to a 'proper standard of

achievement' in a lesser time. The Robbins Committee specifically declared against such an extension; they did not accept as
wholly valid the comparisons that are sometimes made with the
length of study demanded in other countries: our own students
in general come up to the university better prepared and further
advanced; and they doubted whether all students would in
fact benefit from a further year, or would be better fitted for
their future occupations by it. An additional year of study for
selected students after a first degree was thought to be preferable to a general extension to four years, which would certainly prove to be a heavy burden on the public purse. Such a
fourth year could suitably be recognized by the award of a
master's degree.

First degrees are awarded either as 'pass' (sometimes called
'ordinary' or 'general') degrees, or as 'honours' (sometimes
called 'special') degrees. The degree with honours is divided
into three classes, of which the second is generally subdivided
into two divisions. A first class is a mark of very exceptional
merit and is sparingly awarded. In some subjects, of which
medicine is the most noteworthy, it depends solely on the
results of the final examination whether the degree awarded is
pass or honours; but in most subjects the course leading to a
degree with honours is markedly different in content and structure from that leading to a pass degree.

The history, prestige, and effect of honours degrees are
matters of importance for an understanding of current developments in university teaching. When they were first introduced
at Oxford and Cambridge in the nineteenth century, and later
at the civic universities, the intention was wholly admirable:
they provided an incentive to the serious and talented student
to work to the utmost limit of his powers. But it was not
anticipated that more than a rather small minority would be
candidates. The pass degree would still be sufficient for students
who came from the leisured classes of society and for whom
three years of mild and intermittent intellectual activity was a
pleasant interlude in the progress to maturity. Things turned
out otherwise.

The honours course proved to be an admirable training for

the examinations for the higher civil service which were thrown open in 1870: indeed the syllabuses and scope of those examinations were geared to the Oxford and Cambridge honours courses, particularly in mathematics, classics, and history. Then the new grammar schools established after the 1902 Education Act came more and more to seek specialist teachers with honours degrees; and in general, whenever a ready assessment of intellectual ability was needed for a post of some responsibility, an honours degree provided it. Until 1914, nevertheless, the honours candidates remained a minority. But by 1938–9 honours degrees predominated, and in that session 5,262 were awarded as against 4,049 pass degrees; and in 1963–4 the corresponding figures were 18,186 and 7,768. Furthermore, the students to whom the 7,768 pass degrees were awarded included: some who take the ordinary degree *en passant* during an honours course; graduates in faculties such as medicine where there is no separate honours course and where honours of any kind are granted only sparingly; and those who transferred from an honours course or who in their final examinations did not reach an honours standard. It is now only a very small minority of students who deliberately seek to enter a university or are accepted with a pass degree in view. Oxford and Cambridge and most other universities have become universities almost entirely for honours candidates.

Many attempts have been made, but without success, to check the progressive debasement of the pass degree. In its heyday it could give a student some insight into a number of subjects; and if they were well chosen they added up to a reasonably good general education at something appreciably beyond the highest school level; and the student, even if he had not become much of a scholar himself, had at least acquired some respect for scholarship and some inkling of what it is all about. But the pass degree has almost completely degenerated into a congeries of odds and ends of courses with no focal point, or has become a consolation award for the unsuccessful honours student. This generalization, however, does not apply to Scotland, where the pass degree remains academically sound and of good repute; and in

Wales, too, the proportion of pass degrees is higher than in England.

The eclipse of the pass degree would be less to be regretted if many honours degree courses did not have the serious disadvantage of fostering too narrow a specialization: a student spends far too much of his three years in the university in the concentrated study of a single subject in a single department, and far too little in other departments. To this defect the departmental organization of the civic and the Scottish universities has largely contributed. The professorial head of a department of study, with whom in these universities lies the responsibility for the curriculum in his subject, naturally wants as many as possible of his students to become first-rate physicists, chemists, historians, or geographers, as the case may be; and so for entry to his department he expects a considerable amount of factual knowledge, which in turn the schools try to give to their pupils. A bad result of all this has been that, at a time when entry to universities is competitive, specialization is hard to avoid in sixth forms and it penetrates even the lower forms of schools. This is a problem which was acutely analysed in the (1959) Crowther Report entitled *15 to 18*. The general requirements for entrance to universities were indeed intended to give a guarantee of a broadly based education; but for the prospective science student the arts side of the requirements, and for the arts student the science side, can 'be got out of the way' under the existing regulations two or three years before he reaches the university. He then concentrates on the faculty or departmental special requirements and he is committed to one or other of 'the two cultures'. When he goes to the university this commitment is often further intensified.

We must not, however, exaggerate the charge against honours courses and degrees; for there are some facts which tend to be overlooked. First of all, a student's final decision about his honours subject can in some instances be deferred to the end of his first or even of his second year in the university; secondly, as a compulsory part of all honours courses in a single subject, subsidiary or ancillary subjects have to be studied for one or two years; thirdly, in many universities 'combined honours' degrees can be obtained by studying two subjects to approximately the same level; fourthly, the study in depth of a single subject is not incompatible with a broader outlook if the relevance of the main subject is specifically and consciously related to other domains of knowledge, thought, and human experience; and finally, the specialized study of some subjects such as classics, history, economics, English or other literatures, because of their inherent content, is less narrowing than that of others. Nevertheless, when all has been said in mitigation, the fact remains that until recently little success was achieved in breaking down the barriers between departments and faculties, and too few positive steps were taken in most universities to restore breadth.

It is here that we find the significance of the new concept introduced at Keele. The curriculum was planned to lead to an honours degree and was based on four years of study, of which the first is devoted to 'foundation studies' in the humanities, in the social sciences, and in the experimental sciences. This year was designed as a whole to give 'an understanding of the heritage of Western civilization, of modern society, and of the nature, methods, and influence of the experimental sciences'; the object was 'to develop in the student at the outset, some appreciation of the nature and interconnexion of the main branches of university studies', and 'to survey the changes occurring in Western society during the last two centuries, stressing the political, scientific, agrarian, and industrial revolutions and their reflections in literature'. Teachers in all departments participate in the lectures and tutorials in this foundation year, and regularly confer together to ensure that it is integrated and fully co-ordinated.

All students attend the whole of the foundation course; and no matter what subjects they may have previously studied at school, there are no exemptions. During the three later years of the degree course the student pursues not less than two or more than three principal subjects; these are supplemented by a number of subsidiary subjects which occupy one or two years each, depending on the nature of the subjects and the student's earlier acquaintance with them; but it is not open to a student to drop the humanities, or the social sciences, or the physical and biological sciences, immediately after the completion of the foundation year; it is virtually only in his final year that the student concentrates his interests—and then it is on two or three subjects, not one.

It would be quite misleading, however, to think of the Keele experiment as if it were only a matter of a new degree structure. Its real significance lies in the fact that university education was being looked at in a fresh way, that the staff collectively and individually were committed to working out a new approach and reassessing it from time to time, and that the pattern of a student's activities at the university, both inside and outside the classrooms, was thought of as an integrated way of life, to which residence on the campus made a major contribution.

This same air of freedom invigorated the thinking of those who planned the newer universities. All seven of them (Sussex, East Anglia, York, Essex, Kent, Lancaster, and Warwick) have set out, each in its own way, to solve the problem of combining a broadly based education and wide outlook on the world and its problems, with that measure of specialized study of selected fields which will fit the student to play a useful part in a society where general ability to be of use must be accompanied by some particular expertise. The Keele device of the foundation year has not been copied, largely because a four-year course of study (except in the case of foreign languages) was not consonant with UGC policy; but the broad principle which it embodied underlies the general organization of these universities and the new degree structures they have planned.

In place of the hard and fast arrangement of departments into faculties, 'schools of studies' have been set up which cut across the older faculty divisions; and only Kent retains the word 'faculty' at all. Many members of staff teach in more than one school, and some teach in more than one formal 'subject'; departments may still exist, but departmentalism is contrary to the new spirit. Languages, for example, in most of the new universities are not dealt with in separate departments, but in a unified language centre. The first degrees so far are the B.A.

and B.Sc. alone, and at York and Lancaster the B.A. covers science subjects also. The courses of students are planned to lead to an honours degree; there is no pass course, and the pass degree is awarded only to those who fail to reach the expected standard. Some further details may be of interest.

At *Sussex* there are already nine schools of studies, including African and Asian studies, which is something of a novelty outside London. In each school, undergraduates have some particular discipline as their major subject, but they also share with other undergraduates common courses in 'contextual' subjects. The contextual courses occupy up to half a student's time and their aim is to establish links between areas of study rather than merely to juxtapose them. Students reading for the B.A. degree take preliminary courses during their first two terms in three fields, which generally include philosophy and history, both of which are treated for their relevance to the modern world. Similarly, students reading for the B.Sc. degree take preliminary courses in three or four subjects, in which mathematics and the structure and properties of matter are included. Provision is also being made for an arts-science scheme for the study of such topics as 'the development, impact, and role of science in society, and the nature of the creative and inventive processes as they appear in the work of scientists, writers, and artists'.

At *East Anglia* there are now seven schools, including Fine Arts (visual and music). A preliminary examination at the end of the second term tests a candidate's work in broadly based courses designed to introduce him to the principal disciplines relevant to the school he has chosen; and later work in the school covers a wide range (biology, for example, including biochemistry, biophysics, and genetics). In assessing the class of degree to be awarded, specific account is taken of the work done by the student during the whole of his course.

York has a different pattern, in that the organization is not so clearly by schools of studies. A student's interest is broadened in two ways: first, instead of concentrating on a single subject he may (as in many other universities) study two related subjects in a combined degree; and, secondly, he has the opportunity of following 'open courses' on topics that interest him for their own sakes or illuminate his major subject of study. In a two-subject degree, each may be studied to the same depth, but if one is taken as a minor subject it still occupies not less than a third of a student's time. When a student specializes in a language, he must offer alongside it another language which he has not taken at school.

At *Essex* the present eight departments are grouped in various combinations in the three schools of physical sciences, social studies, and comparative studies (which embraces government, political science, literature, and language). Students do not follow courses in subsidiary or ancillary subjects, since each student's scheme of study is planned as a group of closely integrated courses, all of which are equally relevant to each other.

Kent has been launched with faculties of humanities, natural sciences, and social sciences. In each faculty the first four of the nine terms are devoted to an integrated area of study which covers several subjects, and the emphasis is on 'the essential connexions between related topics'. When students have taken their 'Part I' examination, they may transfer to another faculty, and in any case may offer a combination of subjects for the final examination.

At *Lancaster* the thirteen fields of study at present provided (including a unique department of operational research) are divided into four groups of related subjects, each of which is controlled by a board of studies. A 'Part I' examination is taken at the end of the first year and covers three subjects, to which approximately equal weight is given, and students are recommended to include a subject in which they did not specialize at school.

Warwick too has schools of studies, including engineering science and molecular sciences; but every undergraduate, whether in arts or science, is expected to attend a common first-year course entitled 'Inquiry and Criticism', consisting of one lecture and one seminar each week, 'in which the methods of the various branches of knowledge such as mathematics, the natural and social sciences, literary criticism, ethics, and politics will be critically examined'; its object is to give to the student 'a sense of the basis and limits of his own discipline and of its place in the universe of knowledge'.

Most of these universities are only just getting under way, and it will be several years before even they can assess the success attending their new curricula, the new subjects and combinations of subjects they are fostering, and the type of graduate they produce. All is enthusiasm and vigour on every new campus; and many young people are excited by the prospect of going to a youthful university and stimulated by anticipation of a course of study that is not stereotyped. With a dedicated staff, small enough to be in close contact with one another, the pioneering spirit is easily kept alive. The testing time will come when these universities have grown in size towards the 3,000 or 6,000, or more, that they have in mind. Then problems and temptations will arise which are inherent in a large organization with its sheer administrative needs; and if the fresh air now blowing over the academic scene is not to become stale and the sunny auguries for the future not to be belied, a continuous re-examination of what is actually happening will be part of the task these universities have set for themselves.

The development of the ten CATS as new universities with a technological bias will surely be one of the most fascinating aspects of higher education for the remainder of the twentieth century. They served a dour apprenticeship under the wing of LEAS, who inevitably treated them, in matters of academic policy, administration, and finance, as nothing more than the top level of a locally created and maintained system of technical education. Within ten years of their designation as CATS and within three years of their emancipation, they have had placed on their shoulders the task of bringing within the university system a pattern of education which will differ at many points from the traditional one. They are still in the process of formulating their policies for the future with the help of their academic advisory committees. They have had experience already of work for the external degrees of London and the Diploma in Technology, and they have gone a long way in developing their research activities.

Now they stand on their own feet and assume not only the privileges but the delicate responsibilities of moulding their own curricula, of setting their own standards for degrees, and —what in the long run will be the basis on which all their work will rest—of sharing with other universities the wider obligation of maintaining academic freedom. Some of their work will be parallel to, but not in direct competition with, that of the faculties of applied science in other universities; but their departments of sociology, economics, business studies, and administration have the opportunity of developing along quite new lines; already some of them are in the fore-front in making use of audio-visual techniques of instruction; and for certain areas of study their successful experience of sandwich courses, which it would be unforgivable of them to jettison, points the way to a new and potentially fruitful concept of university education in this country. Their policies, practices, and experiments, and indeed their philosophies of education, alongside those of the newer universities founded since 1945, will inevitably react in due course on the older universities.

Methods of teaching

In 1961 the UGC appointed a committee under the chairmanship of Sir Edward Hale to enquire into the methods of university teaching; its report was published in 1964. The questions at issue are two: the methods and the quality. As regards method, there are the two extremes: the formal lecture delivered to classes of varying size, and the tutorial instruction given to an individual student; in between these, there are the larger tutorial and discussion groups and seminars—the terms are used almost interchangeably—conducted in an informal manner. During the Middle Ages there were no printed books, even a hand-written grammar was a rare possession for a student, and teachers depended for a livelihood on getting fees from as many students as they could attract; so there was no feasible alternative to the lecture if students were to learn anything at all. It was in the colleges of Oxford and Cambridge that the tutorial method began to flourish, as the senior members made themselves responsible for giving instruction to the juniors of their own college.

The tutorial has long been the keystone of instruction in the older universities, especially in arts subjects; and so far as the university itself is concerned, attendance at formal lectures is voluntary: a student goes only to those which his own fancy or his tutor's advice suggests. In Scotland, where the college pattern did not develop, the mediaeval lecture system persisted, and large classes are still common in the universities there. Over twelve per cent. of the classes in Scotland in the more popular options are well in excess of a hundred students, and the lecturer is in effect addressing a public meeting. The members of such classes, however, are now often sub-divided into small groups for supplementary work based on the formal lecture they have attended *en masse*; and in all the Scottish universities (and notably in St. Andrews) the importance of the lecture is diminishing in favour of a very much greater element of tutorial instruction.

The lecture system was the main medium of instruction in the civic universities until fairly recently, largely because the number of teachers available was not sufficient to provide much tutorial work. An improvement in the ratio of staff to students has subsequently made it possible to introduce a much greater tutorial element; and though individual tuition is still not anything like as common as it is in Oxford and Cambridge, participation in group tutorials of four to a dozen members has become a regular part of the student's life. The newer universities lay great stress on the provision of tuition in small groups as one of the most valuable means of achieving their educational aims.

Lectures, however, are not to be dismissed out of hand. They are valuable for giving a broad exposition of a topic, for helping students to orientate their own reading, for presenting new material not yet available in text-books, for suggesting points of view which are still on the frontiers of thought, and for the general stimulus they afford to students when the lecturer is a man of eminence in his own field and has skill as an expositor. Lectures are indefensible if they are badly prepared, or badly delivered, or merely hand out material which could easily be obtained from a text-book.

The individual tutorial (called a 'supervision' at Cambridge) has its great value in that it is a personal confrontation of two minds. A good tutor knows his subject inside out, has a mind with a cutting edge, is alert to the good and weak points of a student's effort, and is critical, tolerant, and encouraging by turns. It is an expensive system to run in terms of time and of sheer nervous energy demanded: some Oxford and Cambridge tutors are seriously overburdened by their tutorial duties. It is uneconomical if it is, in effect, no more than a private lecture. It is most fruitful when it is centred round some written work previously prepared by the student. Above all, a tutorial is essentially an intellectual exercise, not a social occasion: its purpose is to strengthen the student's mind and toughen it. Its value and importance differ naturally from subject to subject: there can be little significant conflict of opinion between tutor and pupil about the facts of physics; but much divergence of view where literary, historical, or philosophical values are involved. Its effectiveness clearly depends on the quality of the tutor and of the student; with the inferior student it can be a waste of time for both parties.

The group tutorial, attended by several students and possibly by more than one member of staff, is more than a compromise between the large lecture and the individual tutorial: it is a method of instruction in its own right. If well conducted, so that not only the tutor but all or most of the members of the group actively participate, and students match their own powers with one another as well as with the tutor, it does more than offer a solution to staffing difficulties. There are two risks about this method: the first is that the shy or lackadaisical student may shelter behind his more forthcoming companions and so derive little benefit; the other is that it may carry no one any further if it is not focussed on some written work or on a topic to which students have given some previous consideration.

Only sporadic attention has been paid until recently to the quality of teaching at university level. Stories abound of incredibly bad lecturers and indolent tutors; so do tributes to the great ones who have left a lasting impress on their pupils. A member of the staff of a college or a university is chosen for a variety of reasons: his own academic brilliance and promise, his research interests and publications, his acceptability to his colleagues. It is often taken largely on trust that he will be a competent teacher. Some senior tutors in colleges, or professors in other universities, take some pains to ascertain whether their younger colleagues are doing well at this side of their work and help them to remedy defects. But there is no specific training for university teaching as there is for school teaching.

Probably no formal course in paedagogic methods would fit the requirements of all subjects; but it is now generally agreed that some principles of exposition, of classroom techniques, and of the conduct of discussion groups ought to be brought to the attention of tyros in a positive manner and not left to chance and the gifts of nature. Efficiency in the classroom, laboratory, tutorial, or group seminar is a matter of very great concern to everybody, and not least to the student who is without redress in the matter. Proposals are now afoot, however, for research into teaching techniques at the university level and into the processes of learning by university students.

Newer ancillaries to teaching are also coming into prominence: programmed instruction by teaching machines, language laboratories, and—most exciting and potentially revolutionary of all—television. The use of audio-visual aids, particularly in higher scientific education, has recently been surveyed in the Brynmor Jones Report (1965), commissioned by the UGC. Most universities already make some use of closed-circuit television equipment; but the future holds far wider possibilities, by way of linking universities with one another and with other institutions of higher education, and so pooling valuable resources through the exchange of lectures and scientific experiments and demonstrations. This educational hardware can never be a substitute for personal contact between teacher and student, and can certainly not relieve the student of the need for independent thought. But the new techniques, if imaginatively and boldly applied, could within a decade effect something of a transformation in university teaching.

Examinations, standards, and wastage

Written examinations to test the fitness of a student to be admitted to a degree were introduced first at Cambridge in 1772. Prior to that date, such tests as were thought necessary were conducted orally and had become in most instances quite perfunctory. This mediaeval tradition of oral examination has not been entirely abandoned. The final examination for an honours degree still generally includes a *viva voce* part, which may improve a candidate's position in the class-list but does not of itself worsen it. The number of examinations to which a student has to submit himself during his course varies considerably: at Oxford there are the First and Second Public Examinations; at Cambridge there are two Parts of the Tripos (a term derived from the three-legged stool on which the mediaeval examiner sat to conduct oral disputations). At most of the newer universities also there are Parts I and II to be passed; and at the Scottish and the civic universities generally there are formal examinations at the end of each session and progress tests or 'terminals' in between.

The examining work of a university takes up quite an appreciable part of the time of the teaching staff, in setting examination papers, marking scripts, and deciding upon the results. At Oxford and Cambridge much the greater part of the examining is done by panels of examiners drawn in a rough rotation from the internal teaching staff, consisting mainly of college tutors. Elsewhere (and in some instances at Oxford and Cambridge) external examiners, generally drawn from the professoriate of other universities, are appointed by the university to assist the internal staff. This procedure has great advantages for the universities which employ it: for it makes possible a useful interchange of knowledge and experience about the quality of candidates pursuing a similar kind of curriculum in different universities, and so tends to ensure that standards everywhere are comparable.

What then are the standards for a university degree and for

a class in honours in particular? The vast organizations which conduct the examinations at school level for the General Certificate of Education have evolved their own techniques for standardization. These are based on the assumption that, when thousands of candidates are examined on a common syllabus and answer an identical set of question papers, and when the vagaries of individual examiners have been ironed out, the overall distribution of the marks gained by the candidates will follow the outlines of a well-known mathematical curve. The critical decisions therefore are those which fix the points on the curve which are deemed to indicate the border between fail and pass, pass and distinction, and such like; and these points themselves are so selected as to conform broadly to the known policy and 'expectations' of the Department of Education and Science that such and such a percentage of candidates will pass or gain distinction.

The position in university examining is very different. Even the largest group of candidates in a university is too small for such statistical methods to be applicable; in no course is the syllabus identical for any two universities; and there is no external agency which makes known its expectations about a pass rate. The entire responsibility for its own standards rests with each university, and no privilege is more jealously cherished or more conscientiously exercised. The effectiveness of the maintenance of standards depends upon the collective judgement and traditions of generation after generation of teachers, and upon the care which is taken by older members of staff to guard themselves and their juniors from capricious assessments. This is not a confidence trick played on students and the public by an esoteric group of autocrats: it is a skilled art soundly based on experience.

At the top of the scale is the first class in honours which is the hallmark of a special quality. It is never awarded just for diligence in the accumulation of knowledge alone or for a superficial cleverness, but always requires clear evidence of quite exceptional mental alertness and penetration in the handling of the knowledge itself. The 'first-class quality'—or lack of it—is something an experienced examiner recognizes; and when a whole panel of examiners is agreed that it is being shown in a candidate's scripts or oral examination we may be confident that the award of a 'first' has been fully earned. There is no quota of firsts, however large the group of candidates: they just occur; and if you look in any year at the class-lists of the universities, you should not be surprised to find that, even in the most frequently chosen subjects, not a single first has been awarded. The upper division of the second class is the award given to the candidate who for some reason or another just misses a first. The lower division of that same class is the reward of intelligent and sustained endeavour of the kind which can reasonably be expected from one who has been accepted as an honours candidate. The third class is reserved for those whose achievement has patently not come up to the promise they showed when admitted to the university: their mental stamina may not have stood the pace, they may have lost interest in their studies, or they may have been just lazy; but there could be no sillier mistake than to regard them as the intellectual dregs of the nation: some people very distinguished in later life have left their university with a 'third' or even (at Oxford) a 'fourth'.

If the question is asked whether a first, second, or third at one university represents the same level of ability and achievement as at another, the answer must be that those with experience of examining for degrees in several universities do not find that they are modifying their standards from university to university. Public opinion, however, regards an Oxford or Cambridge 'first' with special reverence. A more difficult question to answer is why, in all universities, proportionately more firsts and upper seconds appear to be awarded in some subjects than in others: firsts in medicine, for example, are notoriously few, while those in chemistry are much more numerous everywhere. The answer may lie partly in differences between the subjects themselves, high quality being more easily and certainly recognizable in some than in others; partly in the fact that when (as is generally the case in departments of chemistry) students are only allowed to continue to the later stages of the honours course if good promise is still being shown, a generous

prinkle of 'firsts' is a natural consequence; whereas in a sub-
ect like the clinical part of medicine, where there is no separate
onours course, many firsts are not to be anticipated. The
uggestion that some subjects are 'softer options' than others is
comforting doctrine, but it is not validated by any evidence.
The whole topic, however, could repay careful scrutiny.

Closely related to the maintenance of standards is the prob-
em of the failure rate or 'wastage', which is matter of general
nterest when so large a proportion of students are aided from
ublic funds. Around fourteen per cent. of students leave their
niversities without a degree or any other qualification: of
hese about one half leave voluntarily or are excluded at the
nd of their first year (and so have not excessively wasted
ublic money); a lesser number leave at the end of the second
ear; but relatively few of those who reach their final examina-
ions fail completely and irretrievably. The wastage per-
entages are lowest in arts and highest in technology: this is
enerally explained on the ground that, since many arts subjects
re a continuation of school studies, the arts freshman has
ewer mental adjustments to make than the budding tech-
ologist.

In other countries the wastage rate is much higher, notably
o in many state universities in the USA, where the obtaining
f a minimum entrance qualification gives a student a right of
ntry to the university and where in consequence as many as
ifty per cent. fall out at the end of the first year. Even taking
he American universities as a whole, forty-five per cent. of
hose who begin work for a first degree fall by the wayside. In
he Netherlands, where there are few obstacles to university
ntry, forty per cent. do not achieve a degree, despite the fact
hat many students spend two or three years longer than normal
n their courses. In France, where (apart from the competitive
Grandes Ecoles) the school-leaving *baccalauréat* qualifies for entry,
he wastage rate is fifty per cent. But in Britain much care is taken
n selecting the most promising applicants for a limited number
f places. All universities have procedures for reviewing the
rogress of students and probing the reasons which underlie
cademic mishaps: no student is excluded capriciously or on

the basis of the judgement of a single teacher. A canvass of university opinion would probably show that leniency and sympathy rather than severity towards student performances is predominant.

Why then is the proportion of failures in Britain as high as fourteen per cent., and is that rate a cause for disquiet? Among the points to be borne in mind in considering the first of these queries are the following: no system of selection can be infallible; some students do not develop as expected and reach their intellectual ceiling before the end of the course; some cannot cope with the responsibility of employing their time effectively; some are distracted by outside interests; some withdraw because of ill-health or for personal reasons. As regards the second query, it is significant that a wastage as low as our own is exceptional and is approached only when entry is selective as in the most highly regarded universities of the USA such as Harvard and Yale, which can pick their students. In the Soviet Union, despite selective procedures, the rate nevertheless is said to be as high as twenty per cent.

Research and postgraduate studies

The disinterested pursuit of knowledge is the mainspring of university research. Your born and genuine researcher derives an intense personal satisfaction from the very process of trying to find things out, and the joy of success is the chief reward he seeks. Since it is one of the fundamental doctrines of universities that knowledge is preferable to ignorance, and is good of and in itself, no area in which human observation and human reason can add to knowledge is excluded from investigation. It is on this ground that researches into the kingly dynasties of the ancient Assyrians, the changes in the pronunciation of French in the eleventh century, the formation and breakdown of mesons, the functioning of the ductless glands, the synthesis of peptide hormones, the analysis of storm surges, and a thousand other topics are all justified. The fact that some topics may interest a wider circle than others, or that some have a more immediate relevance to daily life than others, is beside the point. Faraday's work on the induction of electrical currents was not undertaken with the future electrical industry in view. Rutherford was just interested in the structure of the atom and in finding out whether it could be split; and though he appreciated the immensity of the natural forces involved, the harnessing of nuclear power was not what urged him on. The therapeutic uses of penicillin were almost an accidental by-product of Fleming's routine research.

At the same time, it must necessarily be the case that in some subjects almost any topic of research has a close relationship to practical applications. In the medical sciences, in mechanical, civil, and electrical engineering, in optics or acoustics, in veterinary science or in sociology, for example, there is scarcely any new addition to knowledge of which some profession or some industry or some department of government could not make immediate use to the benefit of the community. This, however, does not mean that even in such fields university research is wholly *ad hoc*, or any the less fundamental in its nature; or that university research laboratories are service stations at the disposal of anyone who cares to submit a problem to them. Those who research in these fields may obtain an additional satisfaction from knowing that their findings will directly affect in some way the well-being of their fellows; this prospect may exert considerable influence on their choice of topic for investigation; and in these fields also it is much easier to obtain the necessary funds with which to prosecute research. But to make utility or easy access to financial support the prime criterion would be contrary to the whole spirit of university research.

It is now one of the important functions of universities to train young people who have suitable ability and the right temperament, in the methods of research. Here, particularly in the pure and applied sciences but not exclusively there, a vast body of experience can be handed on: how you define your problem and reduce it to manageable proportions; how you set about collecting facts, making observations, and assessing their relevance; how you plan experiments to refine and expand your cruder factual material or to test an hypothesis; how you construct, adapt, and manipulate your apparatus, and learn, as it were, to think with your hands; how you assimilate what is of value in the literature of the subject; and how you present and communicate your results in a form which others can understand.

Good research, however, is not something which can be turned on like water from a tap. With patience, dogged industry, and some alertness of mind, almost anyone can amass and record a body of facts, and in some fields that can take one a long way; but significant research depends on a creative imagination which sees an order amid the chaos, and so frames an illuminating hypothesis whose validity can be tested.

It is, of course, far from being the case that universities are the only places where advances in knowledge are made. Humphry Davy and Michael Faraday never went to a university, and there is a long line of distinguished professors of the Royal Institution who had no close connexion with one. At the present time government establishments such as the National Physical Laboratory and the Building Research Station, and the large and sumptuously equipped laboratories maintained by the great industrial corporations, are engaged on research projects many of which are of quite as fundamental a nature as those which occupy attention in universities. But, looking at the picture as a whole, it is true to say that in the field of scientific research the universities form the spearhead, and that in the arts and social sciences they hold an unchallenged pre-eminence.

Research is now the spectacular part of the activities of universities. It was not always so. Until 1914, university research, even in science, was mainly the concern of professors and lecturers aided by a few technicians; and only a handful of graduates stayed on for a year or so to work on a problem and write a dissertation for the degree of M.Sc. At that period the majority of arts graduates who aimed at the degree of M.A. registered on a part-time basis as postgraduate students: a candidate saw his professor or supervisor at relatively rare intervals to discuss the progress of his work, and eventually presented his thesis. If, as was often the case, he lived in a place where library facilities were poor, he had a hard struggle to attain his goal. There was, however, both in arts and science, a steady trickle of students from other universities who somehow managed to get to Oxford and Cambridge for postgraduate work.

Since 1919, however, the number of students doing postgraduate research has progressively increased. A turning-point was the institution in 1919 of the degree of Doctor in Philosophy (Ph.D. usually, but D.Phil. at Oxford), which was at first intended mainly to attract American postgraduate students in all faculties who before 1914 would mostly have gone to Germany. The new degree had a much more important effect for our own graduates, especially in science. Industry became more aware of the usefulness of well-trained research workers in their laboratories, and the universities began to supply them in greater numbers; indeed by 1930 there was a temporary glut of chemists with the Ph.D.

To be accepted as a candidate for the degree, a student must have a good honours degree or otherwise show fitness and potentiality. The period of full-time study is not less than two years after taking a first degree; and in some cases it is necessary to pass a preliminary year, for which an M.Sc. may be awarded. In addition to being trained in the methodology and techniques of research, a candidate must present a thesis embodying a piece of original work which, in the opinion of the assessors, makes a positive contribution to knowledge. This supervision of postgraduate students places a heavy burden on many members of university staffs, and there is a risk that their own original investigations may suffer; but the compensation lies in the fact that it is a genuine mark of prestige to have a body of postgraduates who want to work in one's department. Though an appreciable number of postgraduate students who can do so prefer to transfer to Oxford and Cambridge, most postgraduates work in the same university as that in which they took their first degree; and it was with good reason that the Robbins Committee commented on and deplored this lack of mobility at a stage in a student's career when a breath of a fresh atmosphere could be of benefit.

There are necessary limits to the freedom of the postgraduate to choose the topic on which he will work. The problems on which significant work can be done in science are complex, and in the course of postgraduate training it is unlikely that any one person can add more than a mite to the sum of knowledge; if real progress is to be made, team work is essential. Most university departments of pure and applied science concentrate their research efforts in a few areas within the larger domain which their subject covers; and a postgraduate student can be most effectively supervised if he is prepared to work on some definable aspect of the problems to which the department is directing a major effort. Another important factor tending to restrict the student's choice of problem is the great cost of equipment for research. The days of simple test-tubes, sealing-wax, and string in scientific laboratories have gone, and the cost of a single piece of apparatus can run into tens of thousands of pounds. If it is to be used economically, it must serve the needs of as many workers as possible before it becomes out of date; and the range of problems for which it is useful tends to determine the topics on which a department's postgraduate students will be advised to work. If a student wants to work on another kind of problem, he had better go elsewhere.

It might be thought that the total effect of all this is to narrow the vision of the individual student. To some extent this danger is guarded against by the proviso that, in presenting his thesis, the candidate must indicate its relevance to a wider field. Nevertheless, there are complaints from industry that more should be done, particularly in relating the training of a pure or applied science postgraduate student to industrial requirements, and to the management and decision-making in which he may eventually find himself involved. To this question many universities are now giving attention and with the help of industry itself are providing courses designed to give the student an insight into the every-day conditions in industrial research.

With the institution of the Ph.D. degree, the postgraduate degrees of M.A., M.Sc., and M.Eng. came to occupy a different position in the research structure. They were no longer the only degrees available to the young postgraduate worker, and the able and ambitious student who could afford to stay the year or two longer at the university preferred to aim at the Ph.D. There are now three functions which these masters' degrees fulfil: they meet the needs of postgraduates who do not intend to be candidates for the Ph.D., or who are not accepted for the doctorate course and training; they constitute a preliminary hurdle which the aspirant to a Ph.D. can be required to negotiate; and—a more recent development, of which much more will be heard—they can be awarded mainly on the basis of a written examination in courses of instruction planned to supplement the three-year curriculum for the honours degree.

University research and other bodies

In the sphere of research, universities have important links with other organizations: governmental, charitable, and industrial; and to these sources many university departments are indebted for a very appreciable part of their annual maintenance costs. On the governmental side, we may refer first to the Department of Scientific and Industrial Research (DSIR), which was established as a committee of the Privy Council in 1915, when the exigencies of war made plain our deficiencies in research workers and the weakness of some key industries; one of its main purposes was to foster close relations between universities and industrial needs. In 1919 the Medical Research Council (MRC) was set up, and in 1931 the Agricultural Research Council (ARC), to aid research mainly in universities and apply its results in specialized fields.

The functions of these three bodies were re-examined in the Trend Report of 1963, and action was taken in the Science and Technology Act of 1965. The MRC and ARC remain, but DSIR has been dissolved and three new councils have been established. One, the Natural Environment Research Council, is to look after nature conservancy, the geological survey, oceanography, and meteorology—a group which is coming to be known as the 'earth sciences'. The second, the Science Research Council, is responsible for grants for university research and the maintenance of postgraduate students in science and technology; it also takes under its wing a number of other organizations which provide facilities for universities, the most important of which is the National Institute for Research in Nuclear Science, which plans, constructs, maintains, and administers the very large and vastly expensive nuclear machines which no single university ought to be asked to handle. Alongside these two councils, there is now the new Ministry of Technology, which promotes the application of academic research to industry. The third council, Social Science Research Council, has only just begun to function.

The Science Research Council, like its predecessor DSIR, besides making awards to students, makes grants to individual members of a university staff in aid of their investigations, and it finances for a limited period larger projects which cannot be accommodated appropriately within a university budget. In this latter case the grants are made on the understanding that if the project establishes itself on a firm basis, the university will take it over later as a fixed commitment. This stimulus has primed many pumps. The MRC and ARC also award postgraduate scholarships and fellowships, and make personal grants to members of staff; but hitherto they have been inclined to finance permanent or semi-permanent units and research teams rather than individuals. Help also comes from other government sources by way of research contracts with the Ministries of Defence, Aviation, and Public Buildings and Works, the Central Electricity Board, the National Coal Board, the Atomic Energy Authority, and so forth.

Among the many charitable organizations which assist university research projects, special mention may be made of the Nuffield, Wellcome, Leverhulme, and Gulbenkian foundations, and the Livery Companies of London. The support given by the Nuffield Foundation is particularly noteworthy: in the twenty years following its establishment in 1943 it contributed £16M to university research, including £6M to medicine and science and £4M to social science and education. In the same category of help are the contributions made from their limited resources by the Royal Society and the British Academy. And, as evidence of the international nature of basic research, we can point to the help which has come in very bounteous measure to many universities here from American foundations such as the Rockefeller, Ford, and Carnegie; and every year considerable sums are derived from American industry, not all of which are in the form of contracts for specific pieces of work.

Industry as a whole has a vital interest in university research: in a highly competitive world the results of such research and its applications have a direct bearing not only on the prosperity of individual enterprises but on the well-being of the entire national economy. The large firms and combines, and the forty or so industrial Research Associations, are most enlightened in their approach to this matter. In addition to maintaining their own research branches, they give generous and continuous support to fundamental research, the application of which cannot possibly be foreseen. They contribute liberally to the general funds of the universities, assist the work of particular departments, and establish fellowships for Ph.D. students and post-Ph.D. workers. Between industry and the universities there is much cross-fertilization. When a university is asked to help in the resolution of a current practical difficulty, the investigation of it may raise abstract problems and so lead to basic research. On the other hand, the more general results of university research are readily available to industry, not merely through publication but more importantly through personal contacts. Research leaders from industry keep in touch with university laboratories, and universities are generally agreeable that members of staff, when invited, should accept consultancies with limited commitments to give general advice and keep industry apprised of trends inside universities. When professors lunch with boards of directors, there are dividends for both parties.

Colleges of education

We now turn to quite a different topic. During the nineteenth century, before the passing of the 1870 Education Act, some religious bodies established colleges for the training of young people who would teach in their schools. In 1890 the Board of

Education itself began to set up day training colleges for prospective teachers; and from 1902 LEAS were empowered to
maintain colleges of their own. There are now over 150 colleges for the training of teachers (including nine in Scotland)
of which more than 100 are maintained and controlled by the
LEAS. The total number of students in these colleges in 1965–6
was over 80,000, and the Robbins Committee recommended
that there should be 145,000 by 1980. In addition there are
university departments of education which provide a one-year
course for graduates intending to enter the teaching profession; there were 3,801 students in these departments in 1963–4.
Until 1930 it was the Board of Education which conducted the
final examinations for students in training colleges in England
and Wales. In that year, however, this examining work and the
approval of syllabuses was transferred to ten Joint Boards on
which LEAS, training college staffs, and notably the universities
were represented; but the qualification awarded by the universities to their own graduates in training was unaffected.

After the issue of the McNair Report in 1944, the Joint
Boards were superseded by Institutes of Education, which were
established as university bodies by university statutes. Each
university which had an Institute was now collaborating more
directly with the colleges in its own area; and the syllabuses of
the colleges and arrangements for examinations were subject
to the largely formal approval of the senate of the university.
Though the appointment of staff remained wholly within the
jurisdiction of the maintaining authority, the bonds between
the colleges and the universities were clearly stronger than they
had been: the academic and administrative head of the Institute was a university officer who generally had the status and
title of a professor of education; many more members of the
senate than formerly took a lively interest in the work of the
colleges; and when in 1960 a further year was added to the
two-year course in the colleges, the universities played a
very useful part in formulating a suitable curriculum for the
lengthened course.

The Robbins Committee recommended further steps towards a much closer association. The innocuous proposals that

the training colleges should be called Colleges of Education, and that the Institutes should become Schools of Education, have been adopted; but the fundamental proposal that the colleges should be more fully integrated with the universities, administratively and financially as well as academically, has been rejected at government level. This was partly on the ground that, when the universities themselves were engaged on a major task of expansion, they could not at the same juncture undertake the difficulties of assimilating the colleges. There was also the consideration that the LEAS were unwilling to relinquish control of institutions which they themselves had built up, and in the administration of which they had valuable experience. The measure of autonomy within a university framework, to which the locally maintained colleges had been looking forward, was thus not conceded.

The most important recommendation which has been accepted in principle by all the parties concerned is that selected students in Colleges of Education who have the minimum university entrance requirements should be able to take a four-year course and work for a university degree of Bachelor of Education (B.Ed.). Many universities have now propounded regulations to bring such a scheme into effect. It is anticipated that the four-year course will be planned as a unified whole, and a balance maintained between the professional studies and the more academic parts of the course; that college students may, wherever possible, be brought into the university environment for some parts of their course; that some at least of the teachers in the colleges will be given university status as 'recognized teachers'; and that there will be some useful interchange of staffs.

Adult education and extra-mural studies

The endowment deed of Clare College, Cambridge, (1341) envisages the spreading of learning 'beyond the university'; the statutes of Glasgow (1727) provide for the delivery by the professor of natural philosophy of lectures for students 'without a gown'; and John Anderson's extra-mural lectures ultimately resulted in the University of Strathclyde. The great pioneer of adult education, however, was James Stuart of Cambridge, whose influence through the University Extension movement has been mentioned in connexion with the founding of the civic universities. All universities, except the newest, have long had well-established departments of adult education and extra-mural studies, which arrange and conduct classes and courses, mostly in the evenings, not only in the university city but over a much wider area; and through these departments the universities have worked in close co-operation with the Workers' Educational Association (WEA) since its foundation by Albert Mansbridge in 1903, and with the residential colleges for adult education which have been set up by LEAs in various parts of the country. The full-time directors of these departments have professorial status, or at least are members of the university senate.

The greater part of the work is carried out by full-time and part-time tutors and organizers on the staff of the department itself; but very considerable help is also given in the conducting of classes by other members of the university staff. For the benefit of long-term and serious students, these departments have evolved the device known as the 'tutorial class', which extends over three consecutive years. At these weekly classes part of the time is devoted to a lecture by the teacher and part to informal discussion; and students are also expected to do written work. In the early years of these departments the emphasis was on popular cultural subjects: literature, history, and general science; but later on, economics and economic history came to the fore, and the extra-mural classes played an important part in the education of working-class leaders for political responsibility; now, with the increase in leisure and despite the counter-attractions of radio and television, the motive of personal culture has regained lost ground and the list of subjects offered includes archaeology, international affairs, philosophy, psychology, comparative religion, and the appreciation of music and the fine arts.

Furthermore, new tasks have emerged for these departments to tackle, particularly in the field of continued education for those who have had a grammar-school or even a university education. There is a demand for courses from professional workers of all kinds: from teachers, youth leaders, police officers, magistrates, and social workers; and a demand also for postgraduate refresher courses, especially in science subjects where the advances in knowledge are so rapid. What had begun as a salvage operation for the educationally under-privileged has become a significant part of university work.

In 1964-5 the departments were responsible for nearly 2,500 extension courses, consisting of a number of lectures on a single topic, often given by a team of lecturers expert in different aspects of the subject; for 700 short residential courses; for 2,300 sessional classes, most of which have weekly meetings from September to March under the guidance generally of a single lecturer; and for 800 three-year tutorial classes. In all, about 140,000 students were enrolled. The fees for these courses are merely nominal, and it is only exceptionally that an examination is held or any kind of diploma or certificate issued: here, at any rate, learning is its own reward.

Even when universities are expanded to meet the needs fore-seen by Robbins, there will still be work for the extra-mural departments to do. The demand for continued education is likely to increase rather than to diminish, and the provision of refresher courses in all subjects is only in its infancy. As the educational activities of radio and television expand, and a 'university of the air' becomes something more than a poli-tician's dream, the flexible organization and the experience of these departments are at hand to supply that vital element of personal contact which lies at the root of the educational process.

General

No account of the universities in action would be complete without some mention of three other matters: libraries, pub-lishing, and what may be called community service. The im-portance of libraries to the universities themselves, and to the areas in which they are located, is self-evident; they are the granaries of learning. The Bodleian Library at Oxford and the University Library at Cambridge, which have special privileges under the Copyright Acts, have about three million bound volumes each, in addition to vast stores of learned periodicals and world-famous collections of manuscripts; and London, which enjoys no copyright privileges, has, with its constituent colleges, almost four million volumes. All the larger universities have collections running up to more than half a million, and very few well-established institutions have less than 200,000. Access to these great depositories is available to all who satisfy the regulations which their custodians must of necessity make for their safe keeping; and a system of interchange between the libraries themselves extends their usefulness.

A number of institutions, as part of their function as disseminators of knowledge, have established university presses to publish scholarly books written by members of their own staffs and others. The university presses of Oxford and Cambridge, dating back to the sixteenth century, are amongst the great publishing houses of the world and operate their own printing works; and the profits they make from the extensive commercial side of their enterprises have made possible the preparation and publication of many learned and invaluable works (such as the *New English Dictionary*) which could not otherwise have been financed at all. The much smaller presses of Manchester, Liverpool, Wales, Aberdeen, Edinburgh, London (the Athlone Press), and Leicester, which came into being in this century, are supported by modest subsidies from their universities.

Finally, the universities make a general but important contribution, which is often overlooked, by the service which members of their staffs give on committees at both local and national level. Royal Commissions and innumerable committees set up by government departments to consider and advise on a wide range of scientific, technological, sociological, and educational topics draw freely on university staffs for chairmen and ordinary membership. It is to members of university staffs also that local cultural societies look when they need a president or someone to deliver a lecture or lead a discussion; and few governing bodies of schools of all types are without one or more university members. It is impossible to assess the amount of time expended on all these activities; but they certainly constitute a complete rebuttal of the old aspersion that universities are 'ivory towers'.

National Council for Academic Awards

The right of universities to award degrees is specifically conferred on them by their charters or by statute. But this right is not restricted to them: the power of the Archbishop of Canterbury to confer 'Lambeth' degrees was confirmed by the Peter Pence Act of 1533, and is still discreetly exercised; and St. David's College, Lampeter, which awards degrees, does not have university status.

It was therefore not wholly without precedent that in 1964, in accordance with a recommendation of the Robbins Committee, another body was established by royal charter for the award of degrees: the National Council for Academic Awards (NCAA). Its function is to regulate the award of degrees to students who successfully complete work of university standard in institutions not of university status, including the regional and area technical colleges and possibly the colleges of education. The chairman of this body of twenty-one members has described it as a 'disseminated university'. It approves the institutions, the courses, and the external examiners who validate the standards of the examinations conducted internally by the institutions. To be approved, the institution must satisfy the council about the quality of its staff, its facilities for staff research, its library facilities, its programme of advanced studies, and its arrangements for the social amenities of students. The scope of courses which can be submitted for approval is wide, and includes not only all the technologies but such subjects as quantity surveying, economics, social studies, accountancy, pharmacy, and business administration. Emphasis is placed on full-time sandwich courses, but part-time courses are not excluded. The degrees to be awarded are so far the B.Sc. and the B.A., both of an honours standard; while the Ph.D. (unlike that of universities) can be awarded for work done jointly at the institution and in industry. It seems likely that these degrees, which are intended to implement the Robbins recommendation that there should be 'equal academic awards for equal performance', will become a preferred alternative to the external degree of London, particularly in view of the flexibility of the examination arrangements.

The broad picture is that there are now two avenues to a degree. On the one hand there are the chartered universities, including the former CATs, enjoying a considerable measure of autonomy, awarding their own degrees, and receiving support from public funds through the UGC. On the other hand there are (in the main) institutions maintained and controlled by LEAs whose students will be eligible for NCAA degrees. There is thus a sharp academic, financial, and administrative dichotomy within the domain of higher education. This dual or binary system, as it is being called, is a pragmatic device which with goodwill could be made to work satisfactorily. Unfortunately, a rational examination of its educational merits and defects (which is outside the scope of this book) is being overclouded by the introduction of sociological and political dogmatisms.

3
Students and Staff

WE CAN NOW LOOK MORE CLOSELY at the community of persons who constitute a university, the students and the staff. It is convenient and appropriate to deal first with the students.

Selection and admission

Before 1945 an intelligent pupil who wished to go to a university had no serious problem to face, apart from the often decisive one of finance. There were indeed minimum academic requirements to be satisfied, but there was no lack of places: no college or university was overflowing, and if at the beginning of a session there was an increase over the previous year in the number of undergraduates admitted, this was taken joyfully in almost all institutions as a sign of growing prestige. For most English universities the academic requirement was five approved subjects taken at one sitting in the School Certificate examination and passed at the 'credit' standard; in Scotland a similar performance in the old Leaving examination was accepted. Alternatively 'responsions' at Oxford, the 'previous' examination at Cambridge, or 'matriculation' examinations at London, Durham, and Wales were available. All these have now been discontinued.

The first few years after the second world war marked a great change, to which several factors contributed. In 1945 priority was given to ex-service men and women. For the first time it became necessary to make a selection from those school-leavers who wished to enter, and appreciable numbers failed to secure a place even though they applied to several universities: in this way multiple applications became the norm. Furthermore, the number of pupils staying at school to do a sixth form course increased. But the chief factor which made the expansion of university numbers possible was the increase in the number of awards from public funds; and since these awards are tenable at any university where admission can be obtained, students are not tied to the local university: at the beginning and end of every session there is a criss-cross trek of students north and south, east and west.

This surge towards the universities was not impeded by the raising of entrance standards. Despite the perennial academic Jeremiahs who complain that 'students are not as good as they used to be', the 'pool of ability' showed and still shows no signs of running dry. With the revision in 1947 of the arrangements for school examinations and the introduction of the General Certificate of Education (GCE), the minimum requirement acceptable to universities came to have as its core a pass in two subjects at 'A' level. This represents a distinctly higher minimum standard for entry than the former five School Certificate credits. Even so, competition to gain a place did not diminish. A bare pass proved not to be enough to ensure entry; three 'A' levels have become a common offering; and the DES now estimates that by 1973 this high level will be achieved by 55,700 school leavers. In addition, separate faculties and often individual departments have their own special requirements as regards the number and the choice of subjects and the level of attainment: these are not capricious rulings but are based on experience of the difficulties encountered by students who happen to have been admitted with lower qualifications.

At Oxford and Cambridge, in addition to the general requirements, open scholarship and entrance examinations are held by the colleges in the autumn term preceding entry. The colleges lay great store by this system, since it is they themselves who set the questions and see and mark the scripts. They know the qualities they are looking for and are experienced in assessing not only achievement but promise. The winning of an open scholarship at one of the older universities is universally regarded—and rightly so—as the supreme achievement for a sixth form pupil; and the gaining even of a place is no mean feat in a highly competitive field. The less highly esteemed open scholarships at other universities are usually awarded on the results of the 'A' level examinations alone.

Selection of students has become a matter of prime importance. Three criteria are used: examinations results, confidential reports of heads of schools, and interviews. American experiments in the use of psychological tests of aptitude for university study have not yet found favour here. Examination performances, though far from being a perfect yardstick, are the most reliable evidence available of intellectual attainment at a given time in a pupil's career; prognostically they can be misleading, but when three 'A' levels are taken the results tend to show a good positive correlation with the class of degree eventually gained. School reports depend to some extent on the idiosyncrasies of heads of schools and the care and frankness with which they are written; but, particularly when a dean or other admitting officer knows something of the head, they can provide a valuable assessment of future promise as well as of past achievements. Interviews, if they are to be of any use at all, cannot be perfunctory and they eat badly into the time of members of staff; they are expensive for applicants who come from a distance; candidates may not do themselves justice; and those who conduct the interviews are not always expert in the necessary techniques to do the job effectively. Of the three criteria for selection, interviews are the least satisfactory and many universities now use them much more sparingly than was once the case.

By the early 1960s the flood of applicants, with their multiple applications to different universities, had become so overwhelming that the committee of vice-chancellors set up an organization, the Universities Central Council on Admissions (UCCA), to deal with the problem. This clearing-house was an extension of a device which had long been used for applicants to teacher training colleges. The main object was to sort out applications, so that they could be dealt with in an orderly fashion by universities without either infringing the right of applicants to place universities in an order of preference or the right of universities to accept or reject applicants at their discretion. A preliminary trial for technological courses was made in 1962; the full scheme was applied to all universities, except Oxford, Cambridge, Belfast, and the London medical schools, for the 1963 entry; the CATS were included for 1965; and despite the difficulties arising from the fact that entry to the two older universities is by way of the individual colleges, Oxford and Cambridge joined the scheme for the 1966 entry. The residual difficulty is one of timing. Since the results of the 'A' level examinations are not available until late in the summer, final decisions about many candidates have to be deferred until those results are known; even so, there is a 'clearing-up' process to be effected on the brink of the new session, to match remaining vacancies with suitable but unplaced applicants. This is one of the major arguments for bringing forward the 'A' level examinations to Easter—or for deferring the commencement of the university session to January. Each alternative presents its own intricate problems and encounters much entrenched resistance.

Competition for entry will not be eased until the number of university places more nearly matches the demand. Reference has previously been made to the unfortunate effects of this competition on the curriculum of schools, which feel that they must concentrate on meeting the requirements of universities. The one-third 'minority time' for broader studies advocated in the Crowther Report is absorbed, and specialization encroaches. The universities too are caught in the net. Their choice very largely falls on the good examinee who has been well trained to surmount the hurdles they themselves are responsible for setting up. Gone are the days of the 'good pass man' and of the 'perpetual student', easy-going members of the academic society who just squeezed in and ambled along. The competition does not apply only to the candidates. Universities vie with one another in securing for themselves what they judge to be the best of the available applicants, as if every single entrant ought to be likely to go on to a Ph.D. Yet any student who can now meet what are the effective (as distinct from the minimum) entrance requirements is *prima facie* worthy of the best teaching a university can provide.

How do students decide upon the university to which they would prefer to go? The influence of a favourite teacher, the advice of a headmaster or a careers master, the ideas parents have, reports of their experiences from old boys already at a university, and generally vague notions about the relative academic standing of universities or the quality of their amenities: all these play a part, and often the final choice is the odd result of a mixture of the rational and irrational. One doctrine is assiduously inculcated by heads of schools, namely that it is inherently a good thing not to live at home and go to the nearby university. The brighter pupils who think they may have a chance opt for Oxford or Cambridge as first choice; and there are some, especially in public schools, who would not go anywhere else, though this feeling is much less strong than it was. The women's colleges at Oxford and Cambridge, where entry is ferociously competitive, are the goal of every ambitious schoolgirl and her headmistress; and after them the predominantly women's colleges of the University of London are the next popular choice.

Distributions

What then is the pattern which the student body assumes as a result of all these factors which affect selection on the part of the universities and choice on the part of the applicants? The faculty distribution has already been mentioned in another context in Chapter II where Table 1 gives the relevant figures. There are, however, two other distributions of interest. The first of these is as regards sex.

The higher education of women was not a burning topic until the middle of the nineteenth century. Bedford College for Women was established in London in 1849, but it was not until 1878 that the University of London admitted women to its degrees; and it was the first to do so. John Owens' will excluded women from his college in Manchester, and that barrier was not removed formally until 1871, nor effectively until 1883. At Oxford, Lady Margaret Hall was founded in 1878, Somerville College in 1879, St. Hugh's in 1886, St. Hilda's in 1893, and St. Anne's (formerly the Society of Oxford Home Students, established in 1879) in 1942. Of the Cambridge colleges for women, Girton was founded at Hitchin in 1869 and moved nearer to Cambridge in 1873; Newnham was founded in 1871. Oxford admitted women to examinations in 1884, to degrees and full membership in 1920, and to university teaching posts in 1927. Cambridge admitted women informally to tripos examinations in 1872, and to 'titles of degrees' in 1923; but though women were made eligible for teaching posts in 1926, they were not admitted to actual degrees until 1948.

The number of full-time women students in universities in 1938-9, out of an overall total of 50,002, was 11,634 or 23·3 per cent.; in 1963-4 it was 33,809 out of 126,445 or 26·7 per cent. At the postgraduate stage in 1938-9 out of a total of 3,094 there were 396 women, or 12·8 per cent.; in 1963-4 the number was 2,788 out of 18,754, or 14·0 per cent. The proportions differ from university to university, and there is a notable shortage of places at Oxford, where the percentage is 15·7, and at Cambridge, where it is only 9·7. There is also a marked disparity between faculties: almost two-thirds of the women are to be found in the arts faculties, where they account for 40 per cent. of the faculty numbers; in the faculty of science they account for barely a quarter of the whole faculty numbers, and in technology they are a very insignificant proportion. In medicine the overall proportion of women is kept at about 25 per cent. of the faculty, largely because those responsible for their training still hold the view that through marriage the profession loses their services too soon after qualification to justify a larger part of the annual intake.

Various reasons have been advanced to explain why the proportion of women in universities is of this order. It is said that the career motive is not as obviously pressing for them as it is for men; that there are other congenial callings open to them such as teaching, nursing, or secretarial duties, for which a university education is not essential; that in some callings for which a university education is a preparation, such as law or engineering, it is difficult for women to reach the top; that families do not assume so readily as in the case of sons that a daughter should go to a university; and that a greater proportion of boys secure high marks (notably in science) in the 'A' level examinations on which acceptance by universities broadly depends.

Much attention has also been focussed in recent years on the proportion of university students who come from different social, economic, and educational backgrounds. Many political and sociological presuppositions, overtones, and tendentious arguments enter into the discussion; and imprecise or emotive terms are often used. For example, the position has been provocatively put as follows: 'white-collar workers are 20 per cent. of the population, they produce 40 per cent. of the ablest children, who constitute 60 per cent. of the pupils in sixth forms and gain 80 per cent. of university places'. Or again as evidence of social injustice, rather than as a plea to avoid educational wastage of talent, it is pointed out that at one extreme 45 per cent. of all children of the higher professional groups get higher education, while at the other end only 4 per cent. of all children of manual workers and 2 per cent. of the children of unskilled workers do so. The explanation of figures like these cannot possibly lie just on the surface.

The fullest and most reliable statistics are to be found in the appendixes to the Robbins Report. There are two aspects of the matter which, though closely inter-related, can be distinguished: the economic status of the family from which the undergraduate comes, and the type of school where he has been educated. In 1955 a pilot survey made by the committee of vice-chancellors showed that of students entering in October 1955, 24·6 per cent. came from 'working-class' families, the low figures of 13·1 per cent. at Oxford and 9·4 per cent. at Cambridge being balanced by the 31 per cent. at the civic universities. In 1961–2, according to Robbins, 71 per cent. of the undergraduates in universities came from families of non-manual workers, and of these almost two-thirds came from the professional and managerial groups; of the remainder of the undergraduates (29 per cent.), twice as many came from the families of skilled workers as from the families of semi-skilled and unskilled workers. A somewhat higher proportion of the women than of the men came from middle-class homes.

Despite the increase in the number of university places, the broad pattern does not seem to have changed significantly since the pre-war period, except that the proportion of women from the homes of manual workers has increased almost twofold. There is evidence to show that the proportion of students from working-class homes is higher in faculties of science and technology than in arts and medicine, and higher in Scotland, Wales, and the civic universities than in London, Oxford, and Cambridge. The Robbins Committee made a particular effort to obtain figures which would throw light on these matters; but it must be emphasized that precise figures are not available year by year, since universities do not as a matter of routine concern themselves with compiling dossiers on the family backgrounds of their students. An interesting, though not very surprising fact made clear by the Robbins figures is that both parents of half the undergraduates had stayed at school beyond the statutory leaving age, and that in the case of a further quarter of them one parent had done so.

The first attempt to survey the educational background of university students was made as far back as 1938, when the UGC began (but did not long continue) to publish figures showing the number of students who began their education in a 'public elementary school': the figure for England was 38·6 per cent., for Wales 92·0 per cent., for Scotland 65·7 per cent., and overall 46·4 per cent. This was a very crude yardstick. The more recent figures give the following picture. It is in grammar schools maintained or assisted by LEAs that 78 per cent. of the total grammar-school population of the country is educated, and from these schools come 63 per cent. of the undergraduates; direct grant schools (financed partly by fees and partly by government grants) educate 12·5 per cent. of the grammar-school pupils, and from them come 15 per cent. of the undergraduates; the independent schools (where over two-thirds are boarders) educate about 10 per cent. of grammar-school pupils, and from them come 22 per cent. of university students. The proportion of women coming from maintained schools is higher than for men; and the proportion coming from independent schools (of which there are fewer for girls) is lower. The proportion of undergraduates in faculties of pure and applied science coming from maintained schools is higher than in other faculties. In 1961–2 at Oxford 34 per cent., and at Cambridge 27 per cent. of the undergraduates were from maintained schools; and 53 per cent. at Oxford and 56 per cent. at Cambridge came from independent schools. In London 58 per cent. came from maintained schools and 30 per cent. from independent schools. In the civic universities only 13 per cent. came from independent schools, in Wales 9 per cent. and in Scotland 16 per cent.

Viewed from another angle the Robbins figures show that of students coming from maintained schools 8 per cent. were at Oxford and Cambridge, 16 per cent. at London, and the rest elsewhere; and of students coming from independent schools 38 per cent. were at Oxford and Cambridge, 23 per cent. at London. It would be unjustifiable, however, to assume from these figures that different universities have policy preferences for different types of applicant. Very wisely, the UCCA is chary about publishing figures which would constitute a league-table of preferences as shown by applicants; but figures published by Oxford and Cambridge show that, in relation to the number of applications received, as many pupils are admitted from maintained as from independent schools: if pupils from maintained schools do not apply to Oxford and Cambridge, no one can complain if they do not get in.

The picture of student distributions would not be complete without reference to overseas students, who include such distinguished groups as the Rhodes Scholars (at Oxford), the Marshall Scholars (from the USA), and the holders of awards under the more recently constituted Commonwealth Scholarships scheme. In 1963–4, within the total of 126,445 full-time students, 13,786 or 10·9 per cent. came from overseas, 7,562 being from the Commonwealth and 6,224 from other countries. Of the Commonwealth students, 3,827 were undergraduates and 3,735 postgraduates; of the students from other countries, 2,688 were undergraduates and 3,536 postgraduates. Within the total of 18,754 postgraduate students in our universities, the 7,271 from overseas represented 38·8 per cent., a figure which gives some indication of the high repute of the research facilities in our universities. Similar detailed figures are not available for 1938–9; but in that session there were 5,213 overseas students, who formed 10·4 per cent. of the total student population of 50,002 and included 2,857 from what was then the British Empire and 2,356 from other countries. It is interesting to note that despite the pressure from home students, the flow and acceptance of overseas students has increased in absolute numbers and slightly increased in proportions. It has been the policy of the universities, while maintaining the same standard of entrance for all applicants, not to curtail the proportion of these overseas students, whose contribution to the life of the universities while they are here is valuable and whose influence in later life may be significant in many ways.

Student finances

Of all the changes that have taken place in the last half-century in matters affecting students, none has been more revolutionary than the vast increase in the provision made from public funds for tuition and other fees and for maintenance. Before 1914 the majority of students who went to a university did so entirely at the expense of their parents, who often faced considerable sacrifices to make a university education possible for their children. A very bright pupil might be successful in winning an open scholarship or exhibition at Oxford or Cambridge or one of the endowed scholarships at a civic university; most LEAS offered a few scholarships or made a limited number of loans to young people in their own areas; and some schools had small funds to assist pupils going to a university. Students who were prepared to give a pledge that they would enter the teaching profession could obtain grants from the Ministry of Education to help them to take a degree course and a year of professional training. In Scotland needy students could get help from the Carnegie Trust. But all these awards, even when they did something more than cover the fees, left a great part of maintenance to family resources or private generosity. It is quite impossible to estimate how many students who had the level of ability which would now easily ensure their entry into a university, never even considered the possibility of their being able to do so. Their talents were, of course, not lost to the community, since people of this calibre eventually rose to positions of trust and responsibility in many occupations; but those talents were not fostered at a crucial time in their lives nor brought to their fullest potential.

From 1920 the number of awards was progressively increased by a scheme of 'state scholarships' administered by the Ministry of Education on the results of the Higher School Certificate examinations and additional scholarship papers; and since these awards were on a more generous scale than most university open scholarships, a further scheme of the Ministry was later instituted to supplement the value of such university awards. During the years between the wars the LEAS stepped up the number and value of their own scholarships and grants; and loans fell into disfavour. From 1945 onwards, largely because of the growing need for graduates, the principle began to establish itself that any student who gained admission to a university should not be precluded from accepting a place because of financial difficulties.

The Anderson Report (1960) on university awards recommended an all-embracing national scheme which is now in operation through LEAS. Every student who is admitted to a university is eligible for a grant in accordance with the national scale. Apart from tuition and certain other fees, a basic figure (with adjustments for higher costs at Oxford, Cambridge, and London) is calculated, which covers maintenance, clothing, books and equipment, and travel from home. In 1965–6 the maximum for undergraduates in college, hall, or lodgings in Oxford, Cambridge and London is £370, and elsewhere £340; for students living at home the figure is £275. A further allowance for vacations, and in some circumstances for dependants, may be paid. How much of this maximum maintenance allowance is actually paid to a student depends on the parents' income: the lower the family means, the higher the actual award. Up to a certain limit, the emoluments from scholarships and exhibitions do not affect the award.

In 1963–4 the percentage of United Kingdom students who were receiving grants almost wholly from public funds was 89·9 (at Oxford 91·4, at Cambridge 90·9, at London 83·5, at other English universities 93·4, in Wales 94·5, and in Scotland 85·7). The cost in that year had risen to £31.5M. The number of students getting the maximum basic award differs from year to year, but is now about 35 per cent. It is estimated that if a full award were made to all university students the additional annual cost on present numbers would be a further £10M at least. Students often complain that their grants are insufficient, an opinion with which the ordinary taxpayer finds it hard to sympathize. The standard rate of grant is in fact reviewed periodically by a standing advisory committee, after consultation with the universities who have a fairly shrewd knowledge of what current costs for students really are.

Difficulties do, however, arise. The difference between the full award and that which is actually paid is regarded as a 'parental contribution', on the assumption that the family will in fact be able and willing to expend that sum on behalf of the student. If, as sometimes happens, that assumption is not borne out, the student is hard put to it to make ends meet, especially if he is living away from home; and some good-hearted students regard the grant as an addition to a slender family pool from which they are unwilling to take more than they consider to be a fair share. There is a school of thought amongst students which holds that there should be no 'parental contribution' at all, and would regard the full grant virtually as a wage paid during a period of training—a feckless capitulation to servitude.

As the number of places in institutions of university rank increases, the cost of these awards (and the parallel awards for students in Colleges of Education) is likely to become a very serious and possibly crippling item in the national budget for education. The question has consequently been raised whether grants of this type should be limited to the higher level of ability and promise in the form of scholarships, while the remainder of the students are financed largely by loans. It is pointed out that in the USA there are federal and other loan schemes, and that a student there is expected by tradition to do more to pay his own way than here; and in Western Europe generally it is by way of loan that most students finance their university education, and the granting even of such a loan is not purely automatic or to be had for the asking.

The Robbins Committee gave careful consideration to this question. In favour of loans it can be argued, first, that since a university student as an individual can look forward to a higher income as a result of his education, it is unjust that the whole or even a major part of the education should be paid for by others, no matter how much the community benefits in a general way from the presumably higher quality of service which can be rendered; and, secondly, that since what one gets for nothing is undervalued, students would have a greater sense of individual responsibility and be less inclined to press for 'rights' without regard to obligations, if some repayment had to be made. On the other hand, an outstanding loan is a serious encumbrance when embarking on a career, and fear of the difficulties attendant on repayment could diminish the supply of talent applying for entry into universities, particularly so in the case of women, for whom such a debt would be a 'negative dowry'; and parents would be unwilling for their children to be involved in long-term debts. The Robbins Committee agreed that at a time when many parents are only just beginning to acquire the habit of contemplating higher education for their children, the disincentive effect of a loan system would be undesirable; but that future circumstances may lead to some experiment in this direction. More recently, an ingenious scheme has been propounded for lessening some of the disadvantages by linking the period, rate, and total amount of repayment to the actual earnings of the individual graduate. In view of the progress which has been made in the last half-century towards virtually free education at all stages, the introduction of a loan scheme cannot but appear to be a retrograde step, however necessary it might be thought to be on purely financial grounds. We certainly have not heard the last of this problem: a bout of economic retrenchment could transform the situation overnight.

Vacation work

The university year runs from early October to the middle or end of June and consists of three terms of about ten weeks each at most universities, but of only eight weeks at Oxford and Cambridge. The long vacation in the summer months consequently extends over at least thirteen weeks; and it used to be the expectation of the universities that, apart from a reasonable break for holidays, students would spend this time reading in and around their subject and learning to do intellectual work on their own. Most students are in fact given advice about the use of their vacation time and provided with programmes of reading to guide them; and libraries are kept open. But there is no formal test of what they have accomplished. In Cambridge there has long been a four to six weeks 'long vacation term' for science students, without much formal college supervision; in some other places, a few short laboratory and workshop courses are arranged; students of modern languages are generally expected to spend some time abroad; geographers, geologists, botanists, and zoologists take part in field-work; engineers sometimes go to works to gain experience of industrial practice. Unlike universities in the USA we do not have organized 'summer schools' for which academic credit towards a degree can be gained.

Since 1945, it has become the practice and is now almost fashionable for many students to seek paid employment during the long vacations. For this, several explanations are adduced: the money earned supplements the students' grants; it can provide additional funds to make foreign travel possible; working alongside other people in the outside world is a useful piece of social education for the student; and, in some instances, a student just cannot bear to stay at home for weeks on end, while his brothers and sisters go out daily to their gainful occupations. A survey of the use of vacations by students, made by the UGC and published in 1963, showed that 62 per cent. of undergraduates in faculties other than medicine, dentistry, and veterinary science, took paid employment during the long vacation; and of these, three-quarters did more than four weeks, the median period being over six weeks. Clearly the concept of the long vacation as a time for intellectual work supplementary to that of term-time has worn thin, and a radical appraisal of the situation is called for. The types of work undertaken vary enormously, from the hardest and most exhausting manual labour to selling ice-cream at a beach kiosk. If the work in some way adds to the personal development of the student, not many tears need be shed about it; but when it leaves the student physically tired and induces intellectual flabbiness it is indefensible.

The UGC Report confined itself to inviting universities 'to consider whether they could do more to ensure that students make good use of vacations'. But may not a reconsideration of the whole question of the university year, the number of terms, and their duration, be overdue? During the second world war all science and technological departments organized a full fourth term during the long vacation. A modified version of such arrangements, by redistributing and somewhat increasing the time available for teaching within a three-year course, could, in view of the way they use vacations, be educationally to the benefit of the students themselves and show a more economical use of the physical resources of universities. The major problem would be that of staffing the universities on a sufficient scale to enable every member of staff still to have adequate time for his own research.

Student residence

Where and how students live while they are pursuing their university studies is a matter of educational even more than of sociological significance; for the pattern of daily life outside the classrooms and laboratories can affect not only academic progress but the development of the student as a person. In the annual returns of the UGC, students are classified according to whether they live in colleges and halls of residence, or in

lodgings, or at home. Table 2 gives some figures which indicate for groups of universities, and for the student population
as a whole, how the balance between these three kinds of
accommodation has been changing in the last quarter of a
century. The two striking facts which emerge from these
figures are: first, that the proportion of students living at home
has more than halved and is now less than one-fifth of the total
number of students; and, second, that despite the increase in
the number of students in universities, it has been possible to
raise the proportion of students for whom residence in colleges
and halls of residence is available. Some detailed comment,
however, needs to be made to supplement these broad statistics.

At Oxford and Cambridge the college is for all students the
social and educational focus, and it is important to realize that
in both universities the students who are classified as being in
lodgings are also real and active members of their college:

Table 2: Student Accommodation

col. *a* = 1938–9; col. *b* = 1963–4

	% in college or hall		% in lodgings		% at home	
	a	*b*	*a*	*b*	*a*	*b*
Oxford & Cambridge	54·9	58·3	44·0	39·6	1·1	2·1
London	12·0	22·5	41·2	54·4	46·8	23·1
Rest of England	27·2	32·2	17·5	55·1	55·3	12·7
Wales	18·0	32·9	36·1	55·9	45·9	11·2
Scotland	9·0	14·3	30·5	41·5	60·5	44·2
Great Britain	25·1	31·1	33·2	50·4	41·7	18·5
G.B. men only	21·4	28·9	37·5	52·2	41·1	18·9
G.B. women only	37·3	37·0	19·1	45·7	43·6	17·3

they belong to the 'junior common room' (JCR); they dine
regularly in their college hall, and it is in the college normally

that they meet their tutors; they have easy personal relations with the senior members of the college, who themselves have rooms there and for some of whom (if unmarried) it is their home. Because of recent pressures it is no longer possible for every man to have a 'set' (sitting-room and small bedroom) to himself for all the three years he is at the university; but all students spend at least one year in residence in the college, and the lodgings in which they are accommodated for the rest of their time must be approved by the college. Since the number of students in most of the colleges is around three or four hundred, or a little more, there is a strong sense of belonging to a community which has its own history and a continuous tradition, spreading back through the centuries. Go into the lofty and panelled dining-hall of a college large or small, Balliol, Merton, Oriel, Corpus, or Christ Church at Oxford, or it may be King's, Christ's, Magdalene, Peterhouse, or Trinity at Cambridge, and look upon the portraits of founders, pious benefactors, cardinals, archbishops, prime ministers, statesmen, judges, divines, poets, and men of science; who as a freshman would not feel a humble pride that he now is and will remain a member of a society which has been the nurse of men like these? Small wonder that, for so many, loyalty to one's college is a sentiment that lasts throughout a lifetime; and for a mere trifle one can keep one's name on the college books and return from time to time to a Cambridge 'feast' or an Oxford 'gaudy'.

Apart from Durham, which in its collegiate structure resembles Oxford and Cambridge, the civic universities in England and the universities in Scotland and Wales provide a certain amount of accommodation for students in halls of residence, which, in addition to the study-bedrooms, have dining-rooms, common-rooms, and libraries. The proportion of students so provided for varies considerably. The ratio is lowest in Scotland, where a tradition of student independence persists; but St. Andrews has nearly two-thirds of its students in halls. In London, the university itself makes some provision, alongside that for which individual colleges have responsibility; Royal Holloway and Westfield are almost entirely residential, and Bedford has almost half of its students in halls; Imperial College houses about a quarter of its students, University and King's about a fifth, and Queen Mary about one-seventh. This disparity is no less striking amongst the civic universities: Reading and Leicester have halls for more than half their students, Bristol and Newcastle for about a quarter, and Birmingham for about one-eighth. All these 1963–4 proportions, however, are likely to be modified as present building programmes are implemented. Even before attaining university status, the CATS had begun to build halls for their students.

Halls of residence formed no part of the original intentions of those who founded the civic universities to meet the needs of a local population; nor did the Scottish universities (after the Middle Ages) or the Welsh colleges pay regard to the housing of students. But a growth in the number of students who came from further afield, and the need in particular to supervise the arrangements made for women students, led to the establishment (sometimes starting as semi-private philanthropic ventures) of 'hostels'. It is significant of a changing attitude that the word 'hostel' has fallen into disfavour. Opinion within universities, and in the schools from which the students come, has increasingly stressed the benefit, social and educational, which is derived from residence in a properly organized academic environment. The Niblett Report (1957) on halls of residence, commissioned by the UGC, elaborates on the value to students of living, day in day out, with people of their own age, who have varying backgrounds, interests, opinions, and ambitions; by informal contact they educate each other in areas beyond an academic curriculum. Such an experience, at a critical time in his life, widens a student's outlook and teaches him the need for tolerance; the clash of argument around the coffee cups sharpens his wits and brings him face to face with the necessity of defining for himself his own beliefs and ideals.

Halls of residence are in the charge of a warden, who almost always is a member of the academic staff; it is his influence which sets the tone of a hall. He is assisted by a number of

tutors who generally are junior members of the academic staff.
Although the colleges of Oxford and Cambridge have in-
fluenced the way in which halls have developed, a hall differs
in several respects from a college. Membership of a hall is
quite distinct from membership of the university and is coter-
minous with residence; when a student leaves, his connexion
with the hall is virtually at an end. Furthermore, the tutors have
only general supervisory duties and are not concerned directly
with the academic work of the group under their charge;
though resident, they tend to remain in a hall for only a few
years; they are not often custodians of a tradition. There are
many signs, particularly in the newest universities, that halls
will approximate more and more to the Oxford and Cambridge
pattern; indeed in some places the word 'college' is being
preferred to 'hall' to signify the orientation of policy.

Many questions relating to halls are as yet unresolved. What
is the optimum size? The Niblett Report suggested that 150
was as many as a single warden could exert a personal influence upon; but many halls built since 1957 are greatly in excess
of that figure. Should they be near the university in a city
centre, or located in the suburbs? Local circumstances and the
chances of history have often determined the answer in favour
of the suburbs. Is the ideal arrangement similar to that at
Keele and some newer universities, where the academic and
residential buildings are integrated in a single campus? If the
general population is expected to become accustomed to living
in tower-blocks, why should not students? Or is the concept
of a 'student village' to be preferred? Is it possible to make a
still closer integration by providing lecture-rooms as part of
the residences, as at York? Ought not every student, whether
actually resident or not, to be associated in some meaningful
way with a hall, and ought not every member of staff to have
a clear affiliation with a hall? How rigid should be the time-
honoured segregation of the sexes in separate halls located at
a respectable distance from each other? Many Colleges of
Education are now 'mixed', and in universities the barriers
are crumbling. A few fully mixed halls are to be found, from
Aberdeen to Kent; women's colleges in London are accepting

men; and faint-hearted proposals are heard even in Oxford and Cambridge.

Perhaps the most serious question is that which concerns the proportion of the student body which should be in halls. The view has often been expressed that every undergraduate (including those whose homes are in the immediate vicinity of the university) should have the benefit of at least one year in a hall. This would involve the provision of places much in excess of one-third of the student numbers, since there must be a strong nucleus of second- and third-year students continuing their residence in a hall, if a tradition and a corporate spirit are to be established and maintained. It is estimated that the cost of achieving this ideal for the present number of students, even on the most economical kind of construction, would be at least £30M, and that a further £100M would be needed by 1980 if the Robbins figure for the university population is reached. The realistic question therefore would seem to be whether the present level of about 30 per cent. of residential places can even be maintained in a period of unprecedented expansion. The problem is not made easier by the fact that halls are occupied by students for only thirty weeks in the year at most, and that halls can balance their budgets only by accommodating conferences during the long vacation; but the more halls there are in the country as a whole, the greater will be the difficulty of securing summer lettings to supplement their revenues.

Lodgings are the alternative to halls of residence for students coming from a distance; and it should not be forgotten that there are some who prefer a kindly landlady to community life in a college or hall. Universities have so far insisted that women not in a hall should live in lodgings which have university approval; but except at Oxford and Cambridge such a restriction has not applied to men. The expansion of numbers has brought into being a new type of university official, the accommodation officer, whose main task is not so much to control the residence of students as to compile lists of accommodation of a standard which will satisfy reasonable university requirements. It has been difficult in London and the big cities to keep these lists sufficiently large to meet demands even when some of the accommodation required is only of the 'bed and breakfast' type. Sussex deliberately relied on Brighton, and Lancaster on Morecambe, to meet the need for lodgings. Most of the advantages of going to a university away from one's home town are lost if the lodgings are below a certain standard of comfort and amenity, not conducive to study, and miles away from the university. In recent years there has been a movement amongst students to live in flats, singly or in small groups, with little or no supervision of conditions. This gives students a sense of freedom and maturity; but the chores of looking after oneself in semi-isolation dislocate studies and militate against full and fruitful participation in university activities.

What of the diminishing number of students who live at home and pursue their studies at a nearby university? It is evident that, as compared with students in a hall, they forgo the advantages of mingling freely and continuously (if they wish) with fellow students during all their waking hours. It is often objected that such students have a '9 a.m. to 5 p.m.' attitude to the university: they go to lectures in the mornings, return home like office workers at the end of the afternoon, and take no part in the informal life of the university. This is only a very broad generalization; many 'home students' do in fact figure prominently in the student societies; and the same criticism could with almost equal justice be brought against many students living in lodgings. One of the inescapable difficulties for many home students is the sheer waste of time involved when up to two hours or more a day are spent in travel from home to the university and back; yet some London students are forced to take lodgings just as far away. More serious are the personal strains to which some of these students are subjected, especially in a home where intellectual pursuits are not understood or appreciated, and conditions for study are inadequate. Yet, when home conditions are good, and a student gets understanding and encouragement, he may be better off in every way than if he were in the inferior type of lodging.

Guilds and Unions

We now turn to the corporate activities of the student body. As we have mentioned earlier, the focus of social life at Oxford and Cambridge is the 'junior common room' of each college. There are Unions in both the old universities, but they are private clubs; membership is not (as yet) obligatory; and they are best known to the world at large for their debates. Many men distinguished in public life have found there their first arena in politics; and the presidency of either Union often proves to be the first rung on the ladder of fame.

In the civic universities the student body has charter status as a Guild of Undergraduates, and the elected president thereof generally has a seat on the university court. Associated with the guild, there is usually (though not at York) a building known as the Union which is largely under the control of the students for its routine running. Here there are lounges, dining-rooms, cafeterias, rooms for student societies, assembly halls, and sometimes a theatre space. Good-natured senior members of staff often help by serving on committees, particularly those concerned with catering and finance. The Union is the hub of all informal student activities, and is open in the evenings so that students can make use of its facilities after classes and laboratories are finished.

But, as compared with an Oxford or Cambridge junior common room, a Union is a vast anonymity in which the individual student often feels lost and a non-participant; it is the common complaint amongst the student officers of Guilds that their endeavours to create a real sense of corporate life are thwarted by 'student apathy'; and at presidential elections many do not even trouble to vote. The president himself, however, has almost a full-time job in looking after the affairs of the Guild and the Union, attending the social functions of student societies, and representing the Guild at other universities. A part of Guild activities is the production of a student news-sheet, appearing several times a term, which is sometimes critical of the university authorities, more often of the students' own affairs, and provides a platform for the outrageous or sensible ideas of ebullient youth.

Under the aegis of the Guild there exist many student societies: religious, political, cultural, and departmental. Some, like the debating, dramatic, and musical societies, have a long and continuous history; others are always struggling to survive. The religious societies are generally linked with the various denominational chaplaincies, which play an important role especially where there is no university chapel. Political societies rarely attain prominence, and British students are not prone to wild, unruly, and politically dangerous demonstrations which break out amongst university students in some countries. One annual event, however, is always likely to be a cause of trouble: the 'rag-day', which is organized to collect funds for charities, but at times oversteps the bounds of good taste and decent citizenship. Of more ancient lineage is the Rectorial election which takes place in Scottish universities and, by a tradition which reaches back to Bologna, is an occasion for outbursts of wild spirits which are renewed when the Rector whom the students have chosen endeavours to deliver his formal address.

Health services and appointments boards

The beginnings of health services in universities were modest, starting as a single general medical examination for freshmen in their first or second term. As universities became more dependent on public funds, it was felt to be a part of a university's duty to take steps to ensure that a student's academic progress was not impeded by ill-health. Most universities now have one or more full-time medical practitioners on the staff of their own health service, which has special financial and professional arrangements with the National Health Service. Students can attend at surgery hours, or by appointment, and are covered for treatment in all emergencies. Special care is taken to deal with emotional and psychiatric upsets, to which students are sometimes alleged to be more prone than other people of their generation: love affairs and the onset of examinations account for many of the troubles. Some observers have raised the question whether the very existence of a university health service so readily available may not be inducing a certain amount of valetudinarianism.

It is now established practice for universities to show an interest in the way a student will earn his livelihood. The appointments boards which exist in all universities include representatives of commerce and industry and have a permanent officer of their own who brings openings to the notice of students and effects a link between them and employers. Lectures are arranged to inform students about possible careers; a record is kept of vacancies and of students seeking posts; and representatives of firms come to the university to interview final-year students, tell them about the nature of the work offered, and make a selection from amongst the applicants. Many students, of course, secure appointments on their own initiative; but for a considerable number of them, as for employers, the board, with its experience and skill in matching men and jobs, provides a service of proved efficiency.

Contacts with staff

Students come to the university as boys and girls; they leave as adult men and women. This period of metamorphosis is no more difficult for university students than for others of the same age; but while they are at the university students need something more than intellectual guidance. Freed from the restraints of school discipline, given a heady liberty from continuous supervision, many of them away from home for the first time, less affluent than their contemporaries and mildly envious of them, intellectually sophisticated yet personally adolescent and socially immature, they can easily flounder; and the brashness and aggressiveness or, it may be, the nonchalance and feigned cynicism of some of them, often cloaks a deeper personal uncertainty and malaise. It is here that the pastoral element in a university education is most patently called for. This is a task which cannot just be left to chaplains; it is something in which very many members of staff should have a share.

For the student it is not merely a matter of becoming acclimatized to the pattern of life and work in a university, of disposing sensibly of his time, or of keeping up with his studies. What is involved is his need to have a sense of belonging to a genuine community, the feeling that he is not an anonymous unit. This does not mean that students should be coddled, shielded from every breath of adversity, or have their personal problems solved for them; but unobtrusively, like a good parent, the university through its senior members can help. The relationship between a student and the staff cannot of course be one-sided; it has to be mutual to be fruitful; and one of the recurrent difficulties in effecting this is the shyness, diffidence, or subliminal resentment of the student himself: those most in need of help are likely to be those who are most reluctant to seek it or even to perceive the need for it.

The college system at Oxford and Cambridge reduces the problem of contact between staff and student to a minimum. Elsewhere students in a good hall of residence have ready and easy access to the warden and tutors; and the new types of organization with which some of the newer universities are experimenting are designed to make close relationships inescapable. But for those in lodgings, and particularly in a large university, the situation can be very different; and students living at home do not always get from their parents the kind of help they most need. Contacts in the classroom are fleeting and concerned mostly with academic matters; nor is a laboratory the best place for informal intercourse. The small tutorial group provides a better means, but even this is not enough. Many universities have therefore evolved schemes for assigning at least each first- and second-year student living in lodgings or at home to the care of a member of staff who is guide, philosopher, and friend as well as teacher; and everywhere heads of departments and other members of staff make a point of meeting students informally without any organized system. It is only in these ways that students are saved from being overwhelmed by the sheer size of universities in the modern world.

Postgraduates

So far this chapter has been concerned mainly with undergraduates; postgraduates form a quite separate category in

many ways. Acceptance for postgraduate work is not automatic, even when (as most generally happens) a student proposes to remain in the university in which he took his first
degree. Where the postgraduate course consists mainly of lectures (as is the case for some masters' degrees), a man is accepted if he has a reasonably good honours degree, since for
this kind of course there is no serious lack of places. But where
research is involved and the student wishes to embark on a
Ph.D., the matter is different. The supervision of such a student
calls for a considerable expenditure of time and thought on the
part of a member of staff; and in the pure and applied sciences
laboratory space, equipment, and materials have to be provided. The consent of the head of the department is therefore
necessary, and the topic of the proposed research has usually
to be approved by a faculty board.

Of the 18,754 postgraduate students working in universities in 1963–4, the great majority were men, the 2,788 women
being only 14·9 per cent. of the total; and as will be seen from
Table 1 in Chapter II, science and arts in that order constituted
two-thirds of the total number of postgraduates, while technology accounted for less than one-fifth. Nearly one half are
in London, Oxford, or Cambridge; but, apart from the newest
universities, few have less than 300 and many approach or
exceed 1,000.

For the fees and maintenance of postgraduate students a
number of sources of help are available. The universities themselves set aside funds or have earmarked endowments for
scholarships and fellowships; the Science Research Council
makes about 6,000 awards a year for science and technology;
the DES makes a smaller number for arts and the Social Science
Research Council for social studies; and in certain circumstances LEAS make comparable grants. In 1965–6 the maintenance grant for students in college, hall, or lodgings is £500,
and for those at home £380. Industry also, by formal and
informal arrangements, provides the finance for an appreciable
number. A student working for a Ph.D. is also generally per-
mitted, under the regulations governing his award, to receive
payment for a limited amount of teaching or demonstrating:

this gives him useful experience and is of help to the department.

Residence in a hall, or even in a college, is not usually congenial at this stage in a man's career, and the places there are required for undergraduates. Lodgings and flats are therefore the preferred accommodation, and necessarily so when (as now happens more frequently) the student is already married or marries during his course. Nevertheless, attention is now being given to the provision of halls specifically for postgraduates. In this Oxford (with Linacre House and St. Cross and Iffley Colleges) and Cambridge (with Darwin and University Colleges) have led the way; and some individual colleges, like Clare at Cambridge, also have provided annexes for their postgraduates. Even though they may be technically eligible for membership of the students' Union, the postgraduates play little or no part in its affairs, and for them as a group there is in most universities at present no convenient social focus; individually their main contacts are with their own supervisors and with their fellow students in the same department.

Academic staffing

To many people there could appear to be no happier or more satisfying lot than to be a member of a university staff, pursuing one's dominant intellectual interests, secure in one's post until the age of retirement, adequately if not lavishly recompensed on salary scales common to all faculties (apart from medicine where the rate is higher) in all universities, stimulated by constant association with colleagues in many fields of learning, finding intermittent joy in the progress of successive generations of students, assured of time for scholarly investigations, and free from the clamant demands of the market-place and the personal anxieties of free-lance professions.

Oxford and Cambridge. At the two old universities, because of the college system, the pattern of academic staffing differs very markedly from that at all other universities. Although the university itself appoints professors, readers, lecturers, and demonstrators, it is in the colleges that the main strength of the teaching is to be found. It is the college fellows and tutors who do the greater part of the teaching of undergraduates, and it is from their ranks that many of the appointments are made to the full-time and part-time university posts. When a vacancy occurs for a fellowship in a given subject, the college makes its selection in its own way. It rarely advertises the post and often chooses someone who has been an undergraduate at the college. The inbreeding which this system fosters is not as debilitating as might be thought, since many of those appointed have had a few years experience of teaching in a civic university or in a school. Naturally a college must husband its resources by allocating its fellowships to subjects for which there is the greatest undergraduate demand; and it is only the larger colleges which can afford the luxury of fellowships in the less usual areas of study.

The young fellow, if unmarried, has a set of rooms in college, lives and dines there, and shares in all the privileges and amenities of the senior common room: it has to be an attractive post indeed in a civic university to tempt him away from Oxford or Cambridge thereafter, unless he has personal reasons of his own for the move. Until 1871 he would have had to resign his fellowship on marriage; if ordained, he would then probably take a country living in the gift of the college. All told, there are about 800 college fellowships at each of the two universities, as well as a number of prize fellowships of limited tenure. In course of time the young man may hope to attain other additionally remunerated college offices, as bursar or senior tutor. At first, his main occupation is the tutorial supervision of the work of the college undergraduates, an arduous kind of duty, on which during term he may spend ten to eighteen hours a week. As a member of his faculty in the university he has some committees to attend; there is reading to be done, if he is to keep up with his subject; and he will have his own line of research. If he is also in due course appointed to a college or university lectureship, there are formal discourses to prepare and deliver.

The professorships, however, of which there are about one hundred at both Oxford and Cambridge, are university appointments made by a board of electors specially constituted in each case. Formal notice of a vacancy is published, and the electors, whose decision is final, not infrequently choose or invite someone from another university. As the holder of a chair, the professor has the giving of lectures as his main duty; but in the scientific subjects he will generally have additional responsibilities for the running of a laboratory. A person appointed to a chair, whether from within or from outside the university, is elected into (or retains) a college fellowship, but he does not have tutorial duties in the college. At Oxford each professorship is linked with a particular college and in some instances the association is indicated in the title of the chair as, for example, the Corpus Professorship of Latin at Oxford. At Cambridge the arrangements are more flexible. A small number of chairs at Oxford and Cambridge are designated as 'Regius' professorships, and appointments to them (as to similarly named chairs in Scotland) are made by the Crown, acting presumably on expert advice as to the standing of the man concerned.

A familiar figure in Oxford and Cambridge used to be the graduate who stayed on, possibly with the forlorn hope of a fellowship, but had no official position and earned a living by acting as a private coach to students who felt they needed additional help. He has virtually disappeared. The current problem concerns the people (about 300 in each of the two universities) who hold a university appointment as teachers or members of a research staff, but who have no affiliation with a college, unless they happen also to be asked to help with tutorial or lecturing work on behalf of a college. They play their part in the activities of the department to which they belong, but have no share in the amenities of college life or any voice in the administration or policy decisions of the university unless, as graduates, they happen to be members of one of the governing bodies. The conscience of the two universities is worried by the position in which these 'half-members' find themselves; most of the existing colleges can do little to help, since they do not have the finance or the accommodation to expand the number of their fellows beyond narrow limits; but the situation is being eased gradually as plans for the establishment of graduate colleges are being realized.

Staff in other universities. In other universities appointments to the academic staff are not complicated by a dual system. For the vast majority of people embarking on a career in one of these universities, the initial appointment is to the grade of assistant lecturer (renewable annually for three years or so) or to the grade of lecturer. Most of those who obtain these appointments in pure and applied science will already have taken a Ph.D. degree. Vacancies in the grade of assistant lecturer are usually advertised, and the choice, which is made from amongst the applicants by a small committee of the department or faculty, is normally approved by the higher university authorities without demur. Posts in the lecturer grade are filled partly by promotion of assistant lecturers and partly by advertisement. After three years in the grade of lecturer, the tenure of the post become permanent.

There are no statistics to show what proportion of the appointments to the grades just mentioned are filled by Oxford and Cambridge graduates; but a glance at the calendars of universities shows that, while it is still substantial, it is much less than it was a half or even a quarter of a century ago; and the proportion varies considerably from subject to subject. If there is little inbreeding in civic universities, there is now a great deal of interbreeding. The higher posts of senior lecturer and reader are much less frequently advertised and are generally filled by internal promotion. Though many lecturers eventually attain one of these two higher ranks, the number of such posts is limited by the UGC, mainly on financial grounds, to two-ninths of the total non-professorial teaching staff. The academic distinction between senior lecturer and reader is now rather blurred, and the financial differential is small. Broadly speaking, a readership is awarded in recognition of distinguished contributions to learning of a quality which would justify election to a chair if one were available.

A professorship is generally, but far from invariably, advertised, and universities go to great pains to secure external testimony about the merits of candidates before deciding on an appointment; for so much depends on a wise choice. Until recently there was normally only one professor in a department, and the appointment necessarily carried with it the headship and full administrative responsibility for the entire work of the department. A bad appointment could set back a department for a generation. Now, however, many departments have more than one professor, and policy and development need no longer be left in the hands of a single person. The increase in the number of professorships has come about for several reasons: in the first place, in some subjects, as knowledge advances, a particular branch grows in importance and needs to be in the charge of a person of professorial calibre, even though the department cannot be formally divided; secondly, as the number of undergraduates in a department grows, and the administrative burden of attending to correspondence with schools, of selecting applicants for places, of ordering materials, and of writing testimonials increases, the load becomes too great to be borne by one individual; and, thirdly, the increase in the number of postgraduates demands an increase in the number of people of distinction and experience who can supervise and help them. Nevertheless, the ratio of professors to other members of staff has not kept pace with the expansion of staff as a whole. In 1938–9 holders of chairs were 22·3 per cent. of the full-time staff, in 1958–9 they were 13·5 per cent., and in 1963–4 they were only 12·5 per cent. This worsening of the ratio inevitably means that for a young recruit in the lecturing grades the prospect of reaching professorial rank is less good than it used to be.

All academic posts are open to women, and marriage does not involve resignation of one's post. The great majority of appointments, however, are held by men, except in the women's colleges in Oxford, Cambridge, and London. There is nothing sinister in this. If we look at the proportion of undergraduates who are women (26·7 per cent.) and the still smaller proportion of women amongst postgraduates (14·9 per cent.), it is evident that, however willing universities may be to appoint women, the number of those qualified to hold such posts cannot but be small.

Staff-student ratios

An important consideration in the functioning of a university is the ratio of staff to students: Table 3 gives figures for this on the basis used by the UGC. Three groups, however, are excluded: first, the part-time students (16,528 in 1963–4), whose attendances are not uniform; secondly, the part-time staff (number unknown), whose help varies from an hour or so a week to something more than half-time; thirdly, the universities of Oxford and Cambridge as a whole (both students and staff), because all the 1,200 holders of university lecturing posts combine college work with university work, and it would give a false picture to take account only of the 332 holders of full-time professorships and readerships. What therefore is given in Table 3 is the ratio between full-time students and full-time academic staff (including demonstrators, research assistants, and others) for all universities except Oxford and Cambridge. The UGC, however, has expressed the opinion that the overall ratios at Oxford and Cambridge are not materially different from, and may be worse than, those at other universities.

Table 3: Staff-Student Ratios: number of students per member of staff

	1938–9	1958–9	1963–4
By countries			
Great Britain	10·2	7·6	7·3
England	9·5	7·4	6·9
Scotland	13·9	8·4	8·4
Wales	7·5	7·8	7·5
By faculties			
Arts & Social studies	11·0	8·0	8·4
Pure science	} 5·7 {	7·0	7·0
Applied science		9·0	8·0
Medicine	28·6	6·0	5·0

The broad picture is that since 1938–9 the overall ratio has improved markedly; so have the ratios for each of the countries (except Wales, where it was already favourable) and for faculties other than pure and applied science (which is a disquieting feature of the Table). This statistical improvement, however, does not mean that the academic staff is working at reduced pressure. In the first place, the better ratios reflect the closer individual attention which students everywhere (and notably in Scotland) are getting in tutorial groups; and secondly, the increase in the proportion of postgraduates (from 6·2 per cent. to 14·9 per cent.) has necessitated more supervision of research work. The improvement in the faculty of medicine is due to the fact that prior to the Goodenough Report (1944) much instruction was given by part-time clinical teachers, and that there has been a great change of policy towards the appointment of full-time staff. A more detailed analysis would show divergences between one university and another, depending on the amount of tutorial work undertaken, the particular proportion of postgraduates, and the relative size of faculties in a given institution. Exact comparisons with other countries are virtually impossible to establish; but there is no doubt at all that only in the most fortunate of USA universities is the ratio anything like as favourable as here.

The work of the staff

All members of staff are expected to take an appropriate share in teaching, research, and administration. A young assistant lecturer in a civic university will not be unduly overloaded with formal teaching. At an early stage in his career the careful preparation of even a few lectures each week will keep him well occupied; but in this way he builds up a professional capital which will stand him in good stead in future years, provided he keeps those lectures up to date. He will also have students to meet individually; but on the administrative side he will be asked to do little apart from the setting and marking of examination papers. At the other end of the scale, a professor, no matter how skilfully he delegates tasks to secretarial and technical staff, cannot escape a heavy load of administration in his own department; he will attend meetings of his faculty board, of the university senate, and of some of the many committees of these bodies; he will probably also have considerable outside commitments, as a member of government committees or of the council of a learned society, as a consultant in industry (generally with the permission of his university), or as external examiner to another university. It becomes a major personal decision for him to determine how much of his time he shall devote to such activities, how much to undergraduate teaching, how much to the supervision of postgraduates, and how much to his own research.

It is accepted as a general principle that all members of staff should have available for research about a third of their working time (which, be it noted, is not limited to fixed office hours or bounded by the undergraduate term). During the teaching term the time which can be carved out for research may be little; it is mainly in the vacations that most members of staff expect to make progress with their own investigations; and of this fact account would have to be taken in any possible reorganization of the present three-term academic year.

Study-leave and travel now play a larger part than formerly in the life of the staff. There is no scheme such as is usual in universities in the USA for sabbatical leave which can be claimed as of right. Such formal tidiness does not always work to the advantage of the individual or of the institution, and there are clear advantages in the arrangements made in our universities to suit individual circumstances. If a member of staff needs a period of time uninterrupted by official duties to complete a piece of research, to put his material into final shape for publication, or to spend a term or two in another university to study new methods and techniques, he applies for leave, and when possible the university accedes. Some persons are released more frequently than once in seven years, but at times which are determined by the progress of their work. Universities are also willing to agree to the secondment of staff for a year or even two to help an overseas university in a developing country.

In many subjects, especially in pure and applied science, it is often vital that the reading of published material (which is often subject to delay) should be supplemented by direct personal contact with fellow workers in other institutions, if one is to keep fully abreast with the rapid progress in one's own and allied fields; and to a scarcely less degree the same need is felt in some of the humanities and social sciences. Universities consequently now set aside small funds to assist members of staff to make such necessary journeys, which include informal visits to departments in other universities, attendance at meetings of learned societies in London to read or hear a paper, and participation in international congresses and seminars, which since 1945 have burgeoned in bewildering profusion. These things are not extravagant luxuries; they are the basic essentials for advanced research work in the modern world. During a long vacation a single university may be represented at scientific and other conferences of importance as far afield as Tokyo, Buenos Aires, Hong Kong, San Francisco, Washington, and Moscow, or half a dozen other places. Valuable contacts are also made possible by invitations (especially from the USA) to visiting lectureships for a term or a session, by temporary exchanges of staff with overseas universities, and by lecture tours under British Council auspices.

Finally, a brief mention should be made of the Association of University Teachers (AUT). This body was founded in the 1920s at a time when the uncoordinated 'lecturers associations' were finding difficulty in presenting salary claims to the governing bodies of universities. The AUT, however, is not a trades union, and devotes much of its energies to strictly educational matters, such as entrance requirements and international co-operation between universities. In 1949 it was given the right of direct access to the UGC on salary matters; and its views on many topics have had a quietly penetrating effect in university circles.

4

Organization and Finance

THE ESSENTIALS OF THE CONSTITUTIONAL and administrative framework within which universities do their work are easy to understand. First, there are the written instruments of the constitution; secondly, the statutory bodies to which under the constitution various powers and obligations are entrusted; and thirdly, the officers duly appointed to preside over the statutory bodies or to implement the policy decisions and administer the affairs of the university. We shall take each of these elements in turn and elucidate some of the complexities of detail.

Constitutions

Most universities derive their powers and privileges from a royal charter which can be amended only by the Crown itself. Some universities, however, have their constitutional basis in an Act of Parliament which can be amended only by further legislation: among these universities are Oxford and Cambridge, re-constituted by a series of Acts from 1571 to 1923; the four older Scottish universities, remodelled by Acts of 1858, 1889, and 1966; and London, which now relies on an Act of 1926.

The *charter* (or Act) incorporates the university, confers on it perpetual succession and the right to award degrees, and authorizes it to have a common seal, to sue and be sued, and to hold property. Among other provisions, it also defines what statutory bodies there shall be and with what powers, what principal officers the university shall appoint, and what matters shall of necessity be dealt with by university statutes. It is in the charter or Act that there are embodied such fundamental principles as the university's duty to teach, examine, and prosecute research, the proscription of religious tests, and the equal status of women.

The *statutes* (called 'ordinances' in Scotland) are second in importance only to the charter itself, and they can be amended, rescinded, or added to only with the consent of the Privy Council on the application of the university. They define in more detail the broad provisions of the charter or Act, setting forth, for example, the composition of the statutory bodies (court, council, senate, and such like), the definition of their powers, their relations to one another, and the eligibility and mode of election of persons to serve on them. The separate colleges at Oxford and Cambridge are also governed under analogous statutes, for the alteration of which the consent of the university as well as of the Privy Council is required.

Subsidiary to the charter and statutes there are *ordinances*, *decrees* (at Oxford), *graces* (at Cambridge), and, still further down the scale, *regulations*, all of which either add detail to the statutes or deal with matters, such as entrance requirements and conditions for the award of degrees, which the university finds it necessary or advisable to promulgate for the orderly conduct of its affairs. Provided these ordinances and regulations are approved by the appropriate university body, no further authority has to be sought, and they can be altered whenever it suits the convenience of the university.

The statutory bodies: Oxford and Cambridge

In all universities there is a hierarchy of statutory bodies. First, there is a supreme governing body, most generally called the court, which exercises final control within the limits set out in the charter and statutes; then there are other bodies, such as senates and boards of faculties which regulate the academic work of the university; and still other bodies, often called the council or financial board, which are responsible for financial affairs. Within this broad pattern, however, there is great diversity, and for historical reasons the nomenclature is far from being identical in all universities. We must therefore deal with the universities in groups, beginning with Oxford and Cambridge.

The first thing to stress about the government of the two old universities is that it is absolutely and entirely in the hands of members of the university: there is no representation of any outside authority whatsoever on any of the statutory bodies. Academically and financially, these two universities have the most completely democratic organization in the world. At Oxford the chief legislative functions are exercised by the *congregation*, a large body comprising all resident teachers and senior administrators. But every measure submitted to the congregation has to be initiated by the *hebdomadal council*, a smaller body of twenty-four elected and *ex-officio* members, which at its weekly meetings digests or takes decisions on business coming to it from the general board of the sixteen faculties. It is the chief policy-forming and executive body in the university and in many ways is the centre of power. Financial administration is entrusted to the *curators of the chest*, a mainly elected body of twelve academic persons which must be consulted by the hebdomadal council when finance is involved in its own proposals. But even though the congregation can reject or amend proposals of the hebdomadal council there is also a check on its own authority. When a proposal is passed by the congregation by less than a two-thirds majority it must be submitted to *convocation*, a body to which belong all masters of arts and holders of higher degrees who have kept their names on the books of a college. Yet convocation, though it is in a sense a parliament of graduates, can only suspend proposed university legislation for a limited time. Since most of its members live away from Oxford, it is only on the most controversial issues, such as the abolition of compulsory Latin for matriculation, that more than a fraction of members take the trouble to attend.

At Cambridge the pattern is very similar to that at Oxford. Corresponding to the Oxford congregation the chief legislative body is *regent house*, the members of which are the resident teachers and senior administrators. The small initiating and executive body which sifts the proposals of the general board of the twenty faculties is called the *council of the senate*. It has two *ex officio* members and sixteen elected by the regent house. The body of graduates corresponding to convocation at Oxford is the *senate* (a term which has a very different connotation elsewhere), which functions fortnightly as a forum for the discussion of proposals approved or made by the council of the senate; and in certain cases it acts as a court of appeal. Financial affairs are in the hands of a *financial board*, comprised of a small number of academic persons.

The constitution of these two universities depends for its working on a delicate series of checks and balances which ensure that academic and financial control does not find itself wholly concentrated in the hands of any small group. The Robbins Committee commented unfavourably on the efficiency of this system; but those who operate it argue that the advantages of letting every interested party have his say at various stages in the formulation of a 'university opinion' outweigh the disadvantages of having to contend with resolute obstructors. Nevertheless, both universities have set up commissions of their own to look into their constitutional and administrative arrangements. One of the stubborn facts of the situation is the influence of the colleges; as members of the university bodies, fellows of colleges can prevent the adoption of any policy which, however mistakenly, may be thought to deal injury to the colleges or violate their autonomy.

Statutory bodies: civic and newer universities

The civic and newer universities (with which we here include Durham and Newcastle) present a very different picture. Here the constitutional arrangements took account of the fact that a great many persons and many outside bodies were involved in their foundation and development: they did not evolve from a closed corporation or guild of teachers and students. In these universities the four major bodies are the court, the council, the senate, and the boards of the faculties. The *court* is the supreme governing authority. It is always a large body, in some cases numbering as many as 300; it includes not only representatives of the academic staff and of graduates, but

heads of schools, local members of Parliament, persons nominated by other universities, by local authorities and educational
organizations, by religious denominations, and by local and
national learned societies. Indeed all interests which may be
thought to have some stake in the welfare of the university
have seats on the court. It meets annually to receive financial
accounts and other reports on the work of the university, and
to appoint certain university officers. Though far too unwieldy
to transact any detailed business, its meetings provide an
annual focus for a review of the work and progress of the
university and the reports presented to it have a wide and
influential circulation. In a real sense it embodies that informed
public opinion to which the university is in the long run
accountable.

The much smaller executive body of around thirty persons,
whose main responsibility is the university's finances, is called
the *council*. It confirms the recommendations of the senate for
academic appointments, and its formal approval is still necessary in some places for academic regulations proposed by the
senate. The powers vested in the council by the charters granted
in the nineteenth and early twentieth centuries gave it control
over the senate in all matters. Its rights, however, were rarely
exercised capriciously or onerously, though serious friction
sometimes arose when a senate's recommendation for the appointment of a professor was challenged. More recent charters
rigorously limit or positively deny any rights of the council in
purely academic matters. On the other hand, university councils have increasingly come to place more reliance on the
financial judgement of the senate, and frequently they put at
the disposal of senate a block sum for it to distribute at its
discretion for such things as departmental materials and equipment. The majority in the council consists of lay members
appointed by the court, one of whom is elected generally for
a limited term by the council as its president; a restricted number, sometimes amounting to two-fifths of the total, is drawn
from the academic staff; and some members are nominated by
local authorities. The chancellor and vice-chancellor are *ex
officio* members.

From the point of view of Oxford and Cambridge the strong and predominant lay element in the council is anathema; but those who have had experience of working within such a system of government are convinced of its positive advantages, and this view was supported by the Robbins Committee. The lay members regard it as a privilege to serve the university, and they are zealous for its well-being. Collectively, they bring to the work of the university a knowledge of affairs and a worldly wisdom which no senate would wish to disregard. And at a period when a vast physical expansion is taking place in universities and considerable sums of public money are involved, it is a great benefit that there are these lay members who give generously of their time—and of their often expert knowledge —on committees dealing with planning and building. Nor is it without importance that there should be a body of men of recognized standing in the community who by their participation in the affairs of universities are in a position to defend them from unjust or ill-founded criticism.

The *senate*, of which the vice-chancellor is *ex officio* chairman, is the chief academic body, and even where its recommendations need the formal approval of the council, its decisions on academic matters are virtually final. It approves and co-ordinates the work of the boards of the faculties, makes recommendations for the filling of professorships and other academic posts, and is responsible for the teaching, examining, and discipline of the students. It awards all degrees of the university, except honorary degrees, which alone need the concurrence of the council. Its membership consists of the professors of the university and a limited number of representatives of the other teaching staff. In some of the newer universities there is a 'professorial board' to which are delegated some of the powers normally associated with a senate.

The *boards of the faculties* are the broad base of the pyramid of academic government. Subject to the overriding powers of the senate, they deal mainly with the curriculum and examinations of the faculties into which related departments of the university are grouped. These boards consist of the professors in the departments concerned, together with elected and co-opted

members of the non-professorial staff who now generally pre-
dominate. The number of faculties varies from one institution
to another (16 at Oxford, 20 at Cambridge, not more than
10 elsewhere), according to what happens to be thought a
convenient type of organization. At some of the newer universities 'boards of studies' or 'schools' replace the boards of
faculties.

The charters of the civic universities also make provision for
a body called *convocation* which consists of all the duly registered
graduates; within a single university they now run into
thousands. This body has no powers corresponding to those
of the convocation at Oxford or the senate at Cambridge. It is
entitled to 'discuss and express an opinion on any matter con-
cerning the university'; and in many cases it nominates a
limited number of its members to the court and in some cases
has one or two representatives on the council. In the nature of
the case its annual and other meetings cannot be well attended;
but the members generally receive some form of annual report
on the university and so are kept informed of what is going on.
Several of the newer universities have no provision in their
charters for any such statutory body of graduates.

Statutory bodies: Scotland

In the government of the four older Scottish universities there
is still a notable element of oligarchy. Under their constitutions embodied in an Act of 1889 (modified for St. Andrews
by an Act of 1953, and for the other three by an Act of 1966),
the supreme governing body is called the *court*; but it is quite
unlike the body with the same name in civic universities. At
Aberdeen, Edinburgh, and Glasgow it has only nineteen members, and its composition is no less to be remarked upon than
its size. Until 1966 it consisted of: the rector (who has the
right to preside), the principal of the university (who presides
in the absence of the rector), and the lord provost of the city
for the time being, as *ex officio* members; three 'assessors',
appointed severally by the chancellor, the rector, and the town
council; four members elected by the 'senatus academicus' and
four by the 'general council'. The 1966 Act added two mem-

bers from the non-professorial staff and three to be co-opted by the court itself. There has been a similar pattern at St. Andrews since 1953, but the total number there is twenty-one. It is this body which controls the finances, property, and general administration of the university, approves academic appointments, and can review any decision of the senate against which there is an appeal. It might appear from its structure that it is somewhat remote from the daily life of the university; and the balance of academic, civic, and more general interests is so delicately poised that conflicts and friction could arise within the court itself, and between the court and the rest of the university. It is said, however, that such has rarely been the case, and it is obvious that much depends on the wisdom shown in the choice of the three assessors, the representatives of the general council, and the co-opted members.

The powers and composition of the *senatus academicus* and of the faculties are similar to those prevailing in the civic universities. The *general council*, however, has no exact parallel elsewhere. It consists of the chancellor, members of the court, all the graduates of the university (who have no separate 'convocation'), the professors, and all readers and lecturers of more than one year's standing. This academic parliament meets twice a year, and in addition to electing the chancellor and its own four members of the court, it can send resolutions to the court on matters affecting the university. The constitution of Strathclyde does not differ widely from the traditional Scottish pattern; but the university has no rector, and there are no assessors on the court, which consists of twenty-six members.

Statutory bodies: federal universities

The cardinal principle of the constitutions of the two federal universities of London and Wales is that academic and financial matters which concern the whole university are controlled from the centre, while the constituent institutions manage all other matters for themselves. In London the central body which controls finance is the *court*, whose 17 members include 6 representatives of the senate, 4 persons appointed by the Crown, and 3 persons nominated by local authorities. It is the body which applies to the UGC, local authorities, and other bodies for grants, and distributes them to the constituent schools and institutes of the university. In academic matters the central governing and executive body, largely independent of the court, is the *senate*, which considers and approves recommendations of the boards of the faculties, co-ordinates examinations, and in consultation with the school concerned appoints (with university status) the professors, readers, and all but the more junior members of staff. Its fifty or so members include representatives of the heads of the constituent schools, of the faculties, and of the graduates. Amongst its important standing committees are the academic council and the collegiate council. *Convocation*, which consists of the graduates who have paid a prescribed fee, elects eighteen members to the senate and may discuss and express its opinion on any university matter. A quite unusual point of significance is that its elected chairman is *ex officio* a member of the court and of the senate. Each of the constituent colleges and schools of the university has its own internal form of government, consisting in general of a governing body with lay representation, an academic board composed from members of the teaching staff, and a finance committee.

In the University of Wales the supreme governing body is a large *court* of over 250 members, very similar in composition to that of civic universities, but containing direct representation of the constituent colleges. The finances of the university, including grants made through the UGC, are controlled by a *council* of about twenty members, on which, in addition to the vice-chancellor and heads of the constituent colleges, there are members appointed by the court and by local authorities. Academic matters are in the hands of an *academic board* consisting mainly of representatives appointed by the faculties and senates of the constituent colleges. The guild of graduates is constituted similarly to the convocation of the civic universities and has similar rights of expressing its opinion on university matters. As in London, each of the constituent colleges has its own board of governors, council, and senate, for the conduct of its internal affairs.

Statutory bodies: general

With the growth in numbers of the non-professorial staff in universities and the change in the proportion of professors (who have *ex officio* membership or representation on statutory bodies), the question of the representation of other members of staff on these bodies has assumed considerable importance. Among the lecturers, senior lecturers, and readers are many persons whose knowledge and experience could be of great value. In many universities within recent years it has been found possible, by an amendment of the statutes when necessary, to give non-professorial representation on senate, council, and court. In the newer universities it has been easier to arrange for this kind of representation, especially on the senate. At East Anglia and Warwick there is an *assembly*, and at York a *general council*, which comprises all full-time members of staff, and has the right to elect representatives to the higher bodies and to submit its own resolutions to them. At Lancaster and Essex there are analogous arrangements.

Another problem is arising from the growth in the size of university staffs. The board of a faculty, if every interest is to be fairly represented, can now number more than a hundred; a senate can be almost as large; and even the council tends to increase in size. Inevitably these bodies have to set up their own steering committees to digest the business beforehand and indicate on what points full discussion is advisable or statutory. There are three consequences: first, the machinery of government and administration may be slowed up; secondly, the academic members of an inner committee, even if they serve on a rota, have to devote more and more of their time to things other than teaching and research; and thirdly, the real power tends to pass to the inner committee itself and away from the parent body.

A study of the charters and statutes of the universities will not of itself give a living picture of the way a university works, and of how policy is formulated and put into operation. The strict letter of a constitution spells stagnation. Almost all that is worth while in the sphere of change or innovation arises in the minds of a few individuals who see the need for reform or development. The wind bloweth where it listeth and statutes and ordinances are only the framework within which a policy can be implemented. Here an energetic professor, there a group of members of different faculties, there a dean or a vice-chancellor has an idea which seems worth an airing. It must then 'go through the proper channels', welcomed, criticized, helped forward, obstructed, or killed by faculties and senate. There is no one point at which policy must of necessity originate, whatever may be the machinery of government. In every university ideas can and do percolate both upwards and downwards. There are clashes of opinion, verbal battles, and even academic lobbying; but in the long run what really determines the health of a university is the liveliness of mind, the sense of responsibility, and the measure of co-operation shown by members of the various university bodies.

University officers

The official head of a university is the *chancellor* who is elected for life. At Oxford the choice lies with the convocation, at Cambridge with the senate, elsewhere usually with the court. Until 1945 this office was normally held by a distinguished member of the House of Lords; but more recently members of the royal family and persons of eminence in the arts or sciences, or prominent industrialists and men of business have been elected. The office is mainly honorific, and the chief duties are to preside at meetings of the court or other governing body of the university (except in Scotland) and to confer degrees. Though he is generally *ex officio* a member of the council, the chancellor by tradition takes no active part in the daily affairs of the university; but by his informal contacts with other officers of the university, and notably with the students, his unobtrusive influence can often be felt; and in very exceptional circumstances he may act as a court of appeal. In many universities one or more pro-chancellors are elected for a limited term of years to act for the chancellor in his absence, except in the matter of conferring degrees which then becomes a function of the vice-chancellor.

In the four older Scottish universities, the vestigial office of *rector* is retained alongside the chancellorship. The holder is elected for a period of three years by the matriculated students for the time being; and the riotous scenes associated with his election and installation have, like the office itself, a mediaeval origin and flavour. The choice of rector is entirely in the hands of the students: he may be a person of great distinction in learning or the arts, a politician, a deservedly popular figure, or a transient notoriety; and the list of nominations invariably contains at least one name which is completely outrageous. *Ex officio* the rector is president of the university court, but it is only occasionally that he has the time, inclination, or temerity to exercise his right.

In the universities of England and Wales and the Queen's University of Belfast (but not at Oxford and Cambridge) there also exists by charter the office of *visitor*, which in almost all instances is held by H.M. the Queen in Council. It is the right of the visitor to direct an inspection of the university and its work; but only in the most extreme circumstances would this right now be exercised. At Durham, as at many of the individual colleges of Oxford and Cambridge, the office is held *ex officio* by a lord bishop, at Newcastle by the lord chancellor, and at Kent by the archbishop of Canterbury.

The chief academic and administrative officer is the *vice-chancellor*, who in the civic universities is generally appointed by the council in consultation with the senate and holds office until the age of retirement. He is usually a person who has won his academic spurs as the holder of a chair in a university; but occasionally a distinguished college tutor, a headmaster, or a senior member of the civil service is chosen. At Oxford, Cambridge, London, and Wales, however, the tenure of the vice-chancellorship is for two or three years and the office is held in rotation by the heads of colleges, except in London where a professor is often elected to the office. In Scotland the official title of the corresponding officer is *principal*, and (except at Edinburgh) he is appointed by the Crown. The principal, however, is invariably nominated also as vice-chancellor by the chancellor. The duties of a permanent vice-chancellor are arduous, and his influence, if not his power, is probably the greatest single factor in the well-being of the university. He is chairman of the senate and a member of all its committees; he is *ex officio* a member of the council. He guides academic policy without dictating it; for, having a synoptic view of the work of the university, he is able to harmonize conflicting views and interests, give tactful advice when it may be helpful, restrain hasty actions, and promote what seems to him to be of benefit to the university. He interprets the senate to the council and *vice versa*; he keeps sweet the relations between the students and the rest of the university; he is the official representative of the university on formal occasions, and in a large city can scarcely avoid being something of a public figure. Outside the university, he is often invited to sit on important government and other committees; and further afield he may serve on educational commissions anywhere overseas. Some of the burden is eased by the appointment of one or more part-time pro-vice-chancellors from amongst the professoriate; and a full-time deputy vice-chancellor has been suggested as a possible remedy to lighten the pressure.

In London there is a permanent officer, with the title of *principal*, who shares the administrative and some of the academic duties with the temporary vice-chancellor. At Oxford and Cambridge the question has been raised whether in modern circumstances the short tenure of the office of vice-chancellor by a succession of heads of colleges is in the best interests of the university. Holders of the office will normally have had previous insight into policy matters by membership of the hebdomadal council; but it is not wholly satisfactory that almost as soon as a man has become accustomed to the full responsibility of the vice-chancellorship, he should have to lay the office down. The colleges, however, are jealous of their prerogatives, and everyone fears 'an academic overlord'. In Wales the problem of a vice-chancellorship held in rotation is not so serious, since the holder, as principal of a constituent college, is already occupied full-time in academic and financial administration at both college and university level.

The administrative officer of a faculty (or 'school' or 'board of studies' in the newer universities) is the *dean*, whose duties are to co-ordinate the work of the faculty, select and admit students, and present the business of the faculty to the senate. With few exceptions (mainly in medicine) the office is part-time, and the holder is generally elected annually by his colleagues for a few years; he has nothing like the power or influence of the permanent dean of an American faculty. In large faculties help is given by one or more part-time or permanent *sub-deans*. At Oxford and Cambridge there are no deans of faculties.

At the two old universities there are two *proctors* (a mediaeval office) who are nominated annually by the colleges in rotation. They are best known for their supervision of university discipline; but at Oxford they are also *ex officio* members of the hebdomadal council and the general board of the faculties as well as being curators of the chest.

The chief executive functions are in the hands of a *registrar* ('registrary' at Cambridge, 'secretary' in Scotland), who prepares the official business for the university bodies, keeps the university records, and is responsible for the carrying out of official enactments. He, like the vice-chancellor, has a broad view of all the work of the university, and his knowledge of constitutional and administrative machinery, no less than his personal relationship with the vice-chancellor, are important factors in ensuring the efficiency of the university as a whole. Subject to the overriding control of an honorary treasurer appointed from among its members by the council or the court, the day-to-day financial business and the management of the property of the university are conducted by a *bursar* or *finance officer*. Both registrar and bursar now need the assistance of a large graded staff, and both the administrative and financial sides of university affairs afford the prospect of a satisfying career to young graduates.

The *head of a college* at Oxford and Cambridge is elected by the fellows of the college, though the appointment at Trinity, Cambridge, lies with the Crown, and at Christ Church, Oxford, the head is the Dean of the cathedral. Formerly it was only one of the fellows who was elected by his colleagues, but the choice now often falls on someone from outside.

Co-ordination between universities

The question naturally arises of the extent to which there is co-ordination in the policies and practices of universities in matters of common interest and concern: entrance requirements, the length of degree courses, the development of new subjects, techniques for assessing the recurrent needs of departments, procedures for planning physical expansion, and the control of costs generally, are obvious topics. There is indeed much informal contact effected through members of staff in different universities, which results imperceptibly in the formation of a general climate of university opinion. But the most formally organized co-ordinating medium is the Committee of Vice-Chancellors and Principals (the 'vcs' committee') which meets in London ten or eleven times a year. This committee found itself in being almost by accident in 1918, and at first its infrequent meetings related to business in connexion with government grants. It was, and still is, formally a committee of the Association of Commonwealth Universities, which provides its secretariat; the individual universities, however, now contribute to defray its expenses and they approve its constitution. It consists of all the vice-chancellors and principals of universities, together with the heads of the CATs and a few additional members from Oxford, Cambridge, London, and Wales. Its agenda is concerned with broad points of university policy, and increasingly with communications from government agencies which look to it to give 'a common university point of view'. The Robbins Committee recommended that the vcs' committee should be enlarged to include a further representative from each university elected by the senate for a short term. This proposal (to which no attention has yet been paid) would make the committee a sort of national academic council for universities and completely transform its nature.

The vcs' committee has never been empowered, and has never wished, to speak *ex cathedra* for the universities as a whole; indeed it is punctilious in avoiding any impression that it arrogates to itself any such function: if it did so, the individual vice-chancellors would return home to an irate senate or council. Even when it speaks as a body, as it did in 1962 when the government of the day rejected the advice of the UGC on the amount of grant to be voted by parliament, it makes clear what its position is. Nevertheless it is a body which carries great weight and influence, particularly since 1938, when it had no option but to undertake the task of seeing that the universities were prepared for the possible outbreak of war. Sometimes government departments are inclined to press it to commit universities further than it is able to do. Yet on occasion it takes an initiative of its own. In 1948 it published a study of the planning of halls of residence, in 1958 a study of the qualifications of university applicants, and in 1962 a study of the varying entrance requirements of universities, faculties, and departments. It was the body which studied the problem of co-ordinating applications for entrance and instituted the UCCA. Not least in importance are the contacts it maintains with schools through a joint standing committee. Since 1946 it has organized an annual Home Universities Conference, held in London for a day and a half and attended by four or five representatives of every institution of university rank.

Finance: recurrent expenditure and income

The total recurrent expenditure incurred in 1963–4 by the seventy or so universities and constituent colleges then on the UGC grant list amounted to £102·5M. Since 1963–4 another fifteen institutions have been or are about to be added to the list. The budgets of Oxford and Cambridge were each between £6M and £7M; for five other universities (Birmingham, Leeds, Manchester, Edinburgh, and Glasgow) the sum was in excess of £4M; for another three (Liverpool, Newcastle, and Sheffield) it was over £3M; and only in the case of the four newer universities already on the grant list was it less than £1M. For London, with all its institutions, expenditure ran to almost £28M. Such figures are comparable to the operations of all but the largest industrial and commercial enterprises. Some analysis of the items of expenditure and of the sources of income will throw light on the factors affecting university housekeeping.

Table 4: Expenditure and Income

Student numbers	1938–9 50,002		1958–9 100,204		1963–4 126,445	
	£000's	%	£000's	%	£000's	%
Expenditure						
1. Administration:						
salaries	414	6·2	2,471	4·8	4,691	4·6
other expenses	160	2·4	1,058	2·1	2,187	2·1
2. Departmental mainten-ance:						
teaching & research staff	3,278	49·2	22,901	44·4	44,385	43·4
other expenses	1,076	16·1	12,482	24·2	29,358	28·7
3. Maintenance of premises:						
salaries & wages	101	1·5	2,225	4·3	4,889	4·8
other expenses	693	10·4	4,527	8·8	9,398	9·2
4. General educational costs	239	3·6	2,438	4·7	3,381	3·3
5. Student amenities	71	1·1	763	1·5	1,438	1·4
6. Miscellaneous	446	6·7	2,192	4·3	1,726	1·7
7. Capital costs met from income	184	2·8	469	0·9	849	0·8
Total	6,662	100·0	51,526	100·0	102,302	100·0
Income						
8. Endowment interest	1,036	15·4	1,795	3·4	2,188	2·1
9. Donations	173	2·6	479	0·9	521	0·5
10. Local authority grants	606	9·0	1,501	2·9	1,734	1·7
11. Exchequer grants	2,078	30·9	35,476	67·9	74,500	71·3
12. Other government departments	305	4·6	972	1·8	888	0·8
13. Fees	1,999	29·8	5,739	11·0	9,157	8·8
14. Payments for research	} 515	7·7	{ 3,658	7·0	12,043	11·5
15. Other income			{ 2,653	5·1	3,410	3·3
Total	6,712	100·0	52,273	100·0	104,441	100·0

Table 4 gives comparative figures for the main items in three
separate years. The figures for 1938–9 must of course be read
with the subsequent changes in the value of money in mind;
and all the figures need to be related to the number of students

in each of the three financial years. The items of expenditure call only for brief explanation and comment. *Item* 1: The total cost of administration since 1938–39 has fallen from 8·6 per cent. to 6·7 per cent. The 'other expenses' include printing, stationery, postages and telephones, bank charges, and audit and legal fees. *Item* 2: The salaries of the teaching and research staff are by far the largest single item of expenditure, and one to which a university is committed by the national scales of payment approved by the Treasury. There has been a notable increase since 1938–9 in the proportion which goes on 'other expenses'. These include the wages of technicians (now based on nationally negotiated agreements), the cost of materials and some items of equipment for use in laboratories, and the purchase of books and learned periodicals. *Item* 3: Under 'other expenses' for maintenance of premises, in addition to the actual cost of repairs, there are included rates, taxes, heat, light, water, and electric power. *Item* 4: General educational expenses include the cost of examinations, fellowships, scholarships and prizes, publications, travel grants to members of staff, and part of the cost of extra-mural classes. *Item* 5: The student amenities include the salaries of wardens of halls of residence, the cost of running appointments boards, health services and lodgings bureaux, and grants to student societies. *Item* 6: Under miscellaneous expenditure there are items such as supplements to pensions, subsidies to a university press, canteen deficits, and the cost of ceremonies and hospitality. *Item* 7 covers small building works not included in the UGC capital programme.

The pattern of income requires closer attention, particularly on a comparative basis: for the changes in emphasis are of great significance. *Item* 8: The income received from endowments, whether available for general purposes or earmarked for specific purposes (as almost two-thirds of it is), increased from £1M in 1938–9 to £2·2M in 1963–4, largely as a result of appeals made by universities to the general public; but whereas in the earlier year its relation to the total income was 15·4 per cent., the proportion for 1963–4 was only 2·1 per cent. *Item* 9: Similarly, donations and subscriptions of an *ad hoc* kind fell from 2·6 per cent. to 0·5 per cent. *Item* 10: The contributions from local authorities increased from £606,000 to £1·7M, but the percentage fell from 9·0 to less than 1·7. Local authorities in general seem reluctant, except in the case of newer universities which ride on a surge of local patriotism, to increase direct subventions very markedly: they are responsible for tuition fees and the cost of student maintenance; and for the rest they see no need to do what can be left to the Treasury. The proportionate reduction of their stake in the universities to a fifth of what it was, makes the dependence of the universities on the central government all the more inevitable—and the consequences thereof all the more inescapable.

Item 11: It is in the exchequer grants paid through the UGC that the most dramatic change has taken place since 1938–9. More will be said later about the implications of this figure of 71·3 per cent. for 1963–4; but it may be noted here that virtually the whole of the money involved is for general purposes of universities and very little of it is earmarked for particular needs. It seems unavoidable that as universities increase in size and number this percentage will go up; for, whatever appeals universities make and however great the goodwill they can enlist, none of the other sources of income can be expected to keep pace. *Item* 12: The grants from other government departments include sums received from the Science, Medical, and Agricultural Research Councils. *Item* 13: Income from students for tuition and examination fees (including grants from the Department of Education and Science for the training of teachers) is another source which has fallen rapidly in relation to the total. In 1938–9 it was almost 30 per cent.; in 1963–4 it was only 8·8 per cent.

Fees have been raised from time to time since 1945, partly at the suggestion of the UGC, though some universities (particularly in Scotland and Wales) have regretted any departure from the tradition of keeping fees as low as possible. A raising of fees, however, causes no hardship to the students (almost 90 per cent.) who hold university awards and whose fees are paid through a LEA. The Robbins Committee indeed recommended that the income from fees should be raised to a point where it represented 20 per cent. of the total. No action has yet been taken to implement such a policy, which would mean more than a doubling of the present fees. The ordinary citizen, who notes that the direct grants paid through the UGC and the fees paid through the LEAS (to say nothing of maintenance grants) amount, when combined, to 80 per cent. of university income, may not be greatly concerned about how that total is distributed between rates and taxes; but the Robbins Committee regarded it as a 'source of strength that public finance should come through more than one channel'. With this opinion the UGC and the universities agree; for diversification in the immediate sources of income contributes to freedom in matters of policy. *Item* 14: Of the payments for research, appreciably more than a half are received from government departments in respect of investigations carried out on their behalf. *Item* 15: The final item, 'other income', includes payments for routine tests in laboratories and subventions from bodies which are neither government departments nor local authorities.

Finance: capital projects

The financial involvement of government in university affairs is not confined to recurrent grants but now extends to capital projects. This is a distinctive feature of the post-war period. Before 1939 universities had to look to private benefactions, or to their own small reserves, if they needed a new building: during the whole of the five years before the war only £250,000 was given through the UGC for capital expenditure. But with the need to expand the universities, the Treasury had to face the necessity of helping the universities to provide the necessary buildings; and in 1947 a sum of £20M to be spread over the following five years was agreed to. This was a period of great difficulty in the building industry, and because of shortages of steel and other materials less than £15M was spent on actual building works. After this modest prelude, the programme was accelerated; and every university in the country was able to embark on a large programme of redevelopment. Between 1947 and the summer of 1965 the sum of £198M had been expended on university building works and professional fees, to which must be added £17M for sites and £51M for furniture and equipment, making a total of £266M. In a number of instances the universities have been able to raise funds to supplement the programme financed through the UGC and particularly to erect halls of residence; and for a period those universities which were able to do so contributed up to 10 per cent. of the cost of UGC projects. Since 1965, despite the increasing number of students and the addition of the CATS to the UGC grant list, the rate of development has had to be slowed down for reasons of national economy; nevertheless, a further expenditure of £154M on buildings alone is envisaged for the period from 1965 to 1970.

Cost per student

What is the cost of educating a university student? This is a question which is often asked; and though it is quite impossible to give anything approaching a precise answer, some of the factors involved in seeking an answer may be mentioned.

We can get a very rough and ready figure if we divide the total annual expenditure of universities by the number of students: for the six years from 1958–9 to 1963–4 it works out at £514, £569, £636, £724 and £812. But this basis of calculation neglects the fact that some of the expenditure is not fairly attributable to student costs. Two examples will suffice to illustrate the point: the payments made to universities for research (item 14 and part of item 12 in Table 4) involve expenditure not related to students; and some part—would it be a quarter, a third, or a half?—of the emoluments of the academic staff and of laboratory expenses (item 2 in Table 4) arises not from teaching undergraduates or supervising post-graduates but from research conducted by members of staff themselves. On the other hand, some element of the capital cost of buildings (academic, residential, and social) and of the permanent equipment which students use should be added into the account—but how much? Furthermore, the student costs embodied in university expenditure are not the whole story:

to them must be added the fees (£9M) and the maintenance grants (£32M) paid through LEAs.

Even if it were possible to arrive at a balanced assessment of all these factors, there are other problems: for it is self-evident that not all students cost the same. The equipment needed for an arts student is less than that for one in pure or applied science; and there are unascertained differences between the cost of undergraduate and postgraduate students; nor do we know how much of the cost of educating a medical student is really being defrayed by the Ministry of Health in respect of hospital facilities for clinical instruction. Amid such a welter of uncertainties, who would undertake to pursue the will-o'-the-wisp of a comparison between costs at different universities?

5
Universities and the State

THE THEME OF THIS FINAL CHAPTER is the relationship between the universities and the state, a topic which in recent years has become one of more urgent importance for the universities than ever before.

Autonomy and academic freedom

In any present-day discussion of the nature and functions of our universities, it is a cardinal premise that they are and should remain autonomous institutions and must be allowed to enjoy complete academic freedom, without which not only their status but their effectiveness would be impaired to the ultimate disadvantage of the community. By university autonomy is meant the right of each university to determine its own policy in regard to the admission of students, the appointment of staff, the content of courses, and the standards of degrees. This right is guaranteed in most instances by a royal charter, and in others by an Act of Parliament; it is limited only by the provisions of that charter or Act and by the overriding sovereignty of Parliament. With university autonomy as its foundation, the principle of academic freedom ensures the right of the institution itself and of each member of its academic staff to teach, research, and make public the results of scholarly work in the interests of truth and the advancement of learning alone, uninhibited and unfettered by any extraneous considerations whatsoever.

These are large claims; and in both these regards our universities are more fortunate than some universities elsewhere. A few examples may be cited. In France the school-leaving *baccalauréat* gives a student a right to register at a university without more ado; most academic appointments are within the control of the Minister of Education, who also approves the curricula; and the budget of universities is subject to detailed supervision. In the Netherlands the appointment of professors and lecturers is the prerogative of the Crown, which also makes the appointments to the Board of Curators, who are responsible for the administration of the university. In the Federal German Republic the universities are publicly controlled; professors, while enjoying freedom in their choice of curriculum, are civil servants and are 'called' to their posts by the Minister of Education of the state (*Land*) where the university is situated. In the USA the state universities are under the control of the state legislature; in some of them budgets are approved in detail by the legislature, items of expenditure are subject to a pre-audit check, all purchases must be made through state agencies, and state officials have a voice in the appointment of all academic staff.

A distinction could, of course, be drawn between legal and pragmatic autonomy: as in other operations of government, much depends on the spirit in which the letter of the law is carried out; but the more universities are subservient to whatever government happens to be in power, the less certain is it that the cause of truth and sound learning will be well served. Admittedly universities subject to the kinds of state control just mentioned achieve work of the highest quality; but they do so in spite of the restrictions on their freedom. Universities maintained or controlled by religious bodies (Catholic, Methodist, Baptist, Buddhist or Muslim) are in a special position. They were founded on the clear assumption that certain fundamental tenets are inviolable; and it is logical that in those universities there should be areas of thought where the open expression of heretical opinion is incompatible with the holding of an academic post.

Universities in many countries look with admiration and envy on the autonomy our universities enjoy; but it is not absolute. To go no further back in history, the second half of the nineteenth century was a particularly notable period of university reform through the media of Royal Commissions and Acts of Parliament, to many of which reference has been made in earlier pages. These interventions by Parliament, however, were neither arbitrary nor capricious. In practically every case the commission was appointed only after strong representations had been made by an influential body of opinion within the university itself; and the real purpose of the commission, and of the succeeding Act, was to resolve internal conflicts which could not have been settled otherwise or to bring into effect desirable changes which were technically precluded by an existing charter. Such exceptional procedures differ radically from the continuous control exercised in other countries.

Any current concern about the autonomy of our universities arises not from fear of its abridgement by some decisive legislative act but from the abrasive effects of the increasing financial dependence of the universities on the state. The points at issue are the conditions under which, and the purposes for which, public money is given; and the measure of government control there shall be in the spending of it. It is being argued with increasing emphasis that a national system of education is one and indivisible, that in their undergraduate teaching function (whatever may be said about their research) the universities represent a final or 'tertiary' stage after primary and secondary education, and that the government has a clear responsibility to the community to see to it that the universities, no less than the schools, fill this role efficiently.

Grants in aid

Let us then look at the history of state aid to universities and the present method by which it is administered. Until the end of the first world war, government help to universities was very small indeed. The Scottish universities enjoyed some small grants before the Act of Union (1706), and these obligations were continued as Crown commitments until they were placed on an annual parliamentary vote of £5,000 in 1831. From 1836 a small annual grant of £4,000 was made to London for the administration of its examinations. Requests for aid from Owens College in 1852 and 1872 were not successful; but a grant of £4,000 was given to Aberystwyth from 1882, and a similar sum to the other two Welsh colleges at Cardiff and Bangor when they were founded.

A concerted movement by the English university colleges led to the appointment in 1889 of an *ad hoc* 'committee on grants to university colleges'. This committee of five members (three of them MPs who ensured parliamentary control) were empowered to disburse £15,000, and the eleven colleges on their first list received annual sums ranging from £500 to £1,800. Two conditions were attached: first, that the institutions should publish annual financial statements; secondly, that they should be inspected, not by the committee, but on their behalf by heads of Oxford and Cambridge colleges. Similar *ad hoc* committees were appointed from time to time; and by 1904, when there were 14 colleges on the list, the grant had risen to £27,000. In that year it was doubled to £54,000 and in 1906 to £100,000. In 1906 the first continuing committee—the 'university colleges committee' under the chairmanship of R. B. Haldane—was appointed. This committee itself recommended that there should be a permanent advisory body, and that the grant should be made to the committee itself for distribution and not direct to the colleges. This was a clear foreshadowing of the UGC. Some alarm was felt in the universities and university colleges at this proposal, on the ground that such a committee would become too powerful. Oxford and Cambridge as yet kept aloof and had no share in the grants.

There then occurred an episode in the history of grants in aid which the universities tend to forget—or at least refrain from mentioning. In addition to the exchequer grants, many universities received payments from the Board of Education in respect of teachers in training; and in 1910 the administration of both these sources of income was put in the hands of the Board itself. By 1912 the exchequer grants amounted to £150,000, and the Board's own payments came to an almost equal amount.

By happy chance the Board's committee had as its chairman

(Sir) William McCormick (1859–1930), a graduate of Glasgow and once Professor of English at Dundee. Under his wise guidance a number of principles were firmly established and later were adopted by the UGC. (1) In assessing grants, a five-year period should be envisaged, even though the actual sums were voted each year. (2) The grant should be a block grant, and earmarking should be kept to a minimum: this ensured as little interference as possible with the financial discretion of universities. (3) Favourable note should be taken of local financial support. (4) The committee itself should visit the universities and not delegate that function. This direct and personal knowledge of the work and needs of individual institutions has been the strongest link in the relations between the UGC and the universities. (5) The committee should publish a report on its activities. The early reports set the pattern by dealing not only with the finance under the committee's control but with such questions as professors' pay, superannuation, facilities for research, and libraries. (6) Inclusion in the list of grant-aided institutions should depend on standards of work.

The UGC: membership and functions

In 1918 the prospects for the universities and colleges were alarming. They had made great contributions to the national effort during the war, but their finances were still unstable. The President of the Board of Education (H. A. L. Fisher, a former Vice-Chancellor of Sheffield) therefore called a meeting attended by all institutions of university rank in England, Scotland, and Wales; even Oxford and Cambridge, who had previously had no share in the grants—and had wanted none—felt it prudent to be represented. The outcome was the establishment in 1919 of the first UGC under the aegis, not of the Board of Education, but of the Treasury itself, where it remained—to the great satisfaction of the universities—until 1964, when it was transferred to the new Department of Education and Science (DES). The first UGC had as its stipendiary but part-time chairman Sir William McCormick, whom the universities already had cause to trust and respect. Its other ten unpaid members were academic persons no longer in active service with any university institution. The committee had a semi-amateur and impartial look about it—and so was the less likely to cause alarm in the minds of parliamentarians.

Now, nearly half a century later, it has a full-time chairman and a deputy-chairman; and its members, who are appointed for a limited period by the Secretary of State for Education and Science, number nearly twenty. A majority are professors or other academic personages actively serving in universities; the other members from time to time include heads of schools, directors of education, and prominent leaders of commerce and industry, and there is always at least one woman member. The university members are not representatives of the institutions to which they belong; and the spread of their interests and expertise is such that all subjects are covered adequately. A financial purist might object that in some measure they cannot fail to be beneficiaries of the global sum which the committee as a whole recommends to the Secretary of State, and of the grants it allocates to individual institutions; on the other hand, it is only members of this kind who can have an informed opinion about many of the matters with which the UGC has to deal, and they are appointed in part for their fair-mindedness and sense of public responsibility.

In 1919 the amount placed at the disposal of the UGC was nearly £1M; by 1926 it had increased to £1·5M and by 1938–9 to £2M. Oxford and Cambridge figured in the list from 1922, though they had had interim grants from 1919; but the individual colleges at these universities have never received UGC help. In 1945 the recurrent grant was raised to £5·5M and in 1946 to £9M. It reached £74·5M in 1963–4 and then represented 71·3 per cent. of the total income of universities; for 1964–5 the sum was still higher at £89·6M. From April 1965 the former CATS were included in the UGC list, and the total grant rose to £116·9M in 1965–6. Furthermore, from 1947 onwards, grants for capital expenditure and permanent equipment became a regular feature of the provision made for universities, and over £266M, as we have seen, had been expended for this purpose by the end of 1965.

As the body which is entrusted with the allocation of such

large sums of public money, the UGC is clearly the fulcrum of the entire system of relationships between the universities and the state. Let us look then at their terms of reference. The original 1919 remit was simple and read: 'To enquire into the financial needs of university education in the United Kingdom and to advise the government as to the application of any grants that may be made by parliament towards meeting them'. These terms of reference were amplified in 1946 and 1952 by the addition of the words: 'to collect, examine, and make available information relating to university education throughout the United Kingdom; and to assist, in consultation with the universities and other bodies concerned, the preparation and execution of such plans for the development of the universities as may from time to time be required in order to ensure that they are fully adequate to national needs'. Apart from the authorization to institute and publish factual enquiries (of which the UGC reports on methods of teaching and on the employment of graduates are good examples), the significant changes introduced are, first, that planning is made part of the UGC's functions, and, second, that national needs are the touchstone. From the point of view of the universities, there is nothing here which affects the reasonable exercise of their autonomy; so far from there being any suggestion that they may be told what they must do, they are by implication invited as responsible institutions to share in a consideration of what it is proper for them to be doing in relation to the general good of the community.

UGC procedures

The formal procedures of the UGC for ascertaining the needs of the universities and allocating the available grants between them can be briefly summarized. Towards the end of each quinquennium universities are asked to submit detailed and reasoned estimates of the annual recurrent needs for the following five years. About the same time members of the UGC visit each institution to become acquainted with the feel of the place and to talk separately to every section of the university community: students, non-professorial staff, the senate, and the council. Supplementary visits are also arranged to medical, dental, and veterinary schools. These visits, which are not inquisitorial in intent or tone, or even in a narrow sense fact-finding, provide a background against which the UGC can form a view on the written submissions of a university. Even without the CATS, there are more than 70 separate institutions to be visited, including all the schools of the University of London. This entails a great strain on the time and energy of the officers and members of the UGC; but any radical modification of the system would be regretted by both sides.

When the estimates of all universities have been considered, the UGC assesses what it regards as the reasonable total need and presents its statement to the Secretary of State. Then, when Parliament has agreed a global sum (subject to an annual confirmatory vote) for the ensuing quinquennium, it is the UGC itself which apportions the amounts to the individual universities. The allocations, made in the form of annual block grants, can be used by the university at its discretion; and it is not required that the published accounts of a university shall relate particular parts of its expenditure to the block grant. This quinquennial system, which was viewed with approbation by the Robbins Committee, gives flexibility to the academic planning of a university; but no institution would undertake a major deviation of policy within a quinquennium without consulting the UGC. The grants were made on the basis of the estimates and statement of policy which the university submitted; and if no mention had been made (say) of a new department of chemical engineering, it would be disingenuous of an institution without warning to divert to such an expensive project any appreciable part of its grant made for other declared purposes.

There are two main disadvantages in the quinquennial system. The first is that rises in costs during a quinquennium have to be met either by undesirable economies or by supplementary grants. The second is that in the last year of the period, universities cannot plan with confidence until their allocation for the next five years has been announced. It has been suggested that such difficulties could be minimized if, without resorting to annual grants, quinquennia could in some way overlap each other.

As regards capital grants, the UGC control is more detailed. Parliament agrees to a global sum for such purposes. Until recently such grants were announced only two or at the most three years in advance—which is none too long a period for the planning of complicated academic buildings. Each university submits a list of projects in an order of priority, and the UGC approves for grant purposes this, that, or the other project for starting in a given year. An architectural division of the UGC secretariat keeps watch on certain details. It does not interfere with matters of architectural style or design; but standards of permissible cost per square foot are defined for the particular kind of building (classrooms, lecture-rooms, laboratories, offices, and halls of residence); and the allocation of space for the different types of accommodation is also strictly controlled. The cost of equipment for a new building is also carefully assessed by a specially appointed panel of experts before a grant is made.

How, it may be asked, does the planning function of the UGC operate? On the formal side there are three means which the committee has at its disposal. The first is the positive one of offering incentives. If the UGC feels that a need is not being met, it invites a few or all universities to consider whether, if the necessary funds were forthcoming, they would be willing to do something to fill the gap. Much of the great expansion in pure and applied science since the war has been brought about in this way: the UGC was the channel through which the attention of the universities was directed to this national need. This technique has been used also in connexion with the reports of committees appointed to survey the provision for Slavonic studies, social studies, medicine, and dentistry. Provided the proposed development is academically tolerable, the promise of money is hard to resist. A university could refuse; but it generally finds good reasons for accepting.

The second method of planning control is a negative one through recurrent grants. From time to time the UGC indicates that, in fixing its allocation, some item or other in the estimates of a university 'has not been taken into account'. This means that while the development is not vetoed, the UGC does not approve of public money being used for the purpose. It is then for the university to decide whether it will go ahead out of its other sources of income, in the hope that by the end of the quinquennium the project will have proved its worth and the UGC will be more favourable next time.

The third method is by the selection of projects which universities submit for capital expenditure on new buildings. The giving of approval for a new physics laboratory, and the withholding of it for the extension of an arts building, inevitably determines the order in which a university is to expand not only physically but academically as well.

The importance and strength of the UGC, however, do not lie solely in its formal activities. The basis of its undoubted success as a constitutional device is that throughout the fifty years of its history it has earned and still enjoys the confidence of both the government and the universities. This has been due to the quality of its membership, a succession of enlightened chairmen, and the committee's intimate knowledge of government policy on the one hand, and of university opinion on the other. It is in a position therefore to tender informal advice when needed, to interpret the universities and government departments to one another, to give a friendly nudge this way or that, and to minimize possible causes of friction, especially when, as must sometimes happen, grants are not thought to match university needs.

From its inception until 1964, the UGC was responsible to the Treasury and tendered its advice on the total amount of grant required to the Chancellor of the Exchequer, without the mediation of another Minister. This was thought to put the universities in a very strong position. But as the amount of money for which the Treasury was asked increased, the situation became embarrassing to the Chancellor. In regard to all other departments of state he was the guardian of the public purse, and it was his function to press for the pruning of estimates and not himself to indulge in liberality. An exception could be made for a matter of £5M; but with £50M at stake the illogicality of the position was plain for all to see. On the other hand, when the Chancellor—as notoriously happened in 1962—judged it prudent not to accept the recommendation of the UGC, the universities had no one else to plead their case with the Chancellor himself or with the Cabinet.

The Robbins Committee saw this dilemma and (with one dissentient) recommended that, alongside the Minister of Education, there should be a Minister of Arts and Science responsible for the UGC and the Research Councils, an arrangement which would apparently have been welcome to the universities themselves. In the upshot a unified Department of Education and Science was established with an overall responsibility for education; and to that new department the UGC was transferred in 1964. What effect this will have on the universities in the long run depends on two things: first, on whether the UGC remains a body so constituted as to retain the confidence of the universities, and a body whose judgement and advice are sought and acted upon by the DES; and, secondly, on whether the DES in its day-to-day operations, either through the UGC or by other means, appreciates that in universities the teaching is of a special order, and that the research side is so interwoven with other activities that universities must at very many points be treated quite differently from other parts of the educational system. The Treasury did not claim to have experts in educational matters; the DES is full of them.

The six freedoms

The last few pages have been a necessary background to a discussion of the autonomy and freedoms which are of importance to universities. On this question in general, the Robbins Committee made one of the most significant and fundamental comments in the whole of their report. 'Freedom of institutions', they wrote, 'as well as individual freedom is an essential constituent of a free society and the tradition of academic freedom in this country has deep roots in the whole history of our people. We are convinced also that such freedom is a necessary condition of the highest efficiency and the proper progress of academic institutions, and that encroachments upon their liberty, in the supposed interests of greater efficiency, would in fact diminish their efficiency and stultify their development.' To this they added: 'We believe that a system that aims at the maximum of independence compatible with the necessary degree of public control is good in itself, as reflecting the ultimate values of a free society.' In its quinquennial survey entitled *University Development* 1957–62 (published in 1964), the UGC expressed a similar opinion: 'The justification for such autonomy, in our view, arises from the belief that if the optimum use is to be made of their resources in terms of both manpower and money, decisions in these matters are best made in the universities themselves, by whom the individual circumstances are better known and evaluated than by any outside body.

The UGC gave precision to this generality by specifying six areas in which they believed 'the universities should have a wide measure of self-determination'. It will be noted that it was not absolute freedom but a 'wide measure' of it, to which the UGC was lending its support; and in practical terms the points that could be at issue are: first, the advantage a particular freedom brings to the universities and to the community; second, the sense of public responsibility the universities show in the exercise of their freedoms; and third, what limitation of those freedoms may be necessary in the common interest.

We will now consider as briefly as possible these six freedoms, using the phraseology of the UGC itself as our sub-headings.

1. *The selection of students*. This and the next two freedoms are concerned with the right of universities to determine 'who shall teach what to whom'. Taken together, these three form the hard core of university autonomy: without any one of them the universities could become instruments of government policy and tools for a debilitating form of social engineering.

It conforms to plain common sense that, as a place of learning, a university should admit only those students who on academic grounds are suitable and reject those who are not. The university is the only body which can say what level of academic attainment on entry is necessary if its own standard for a first degree is to be reached in a reasonable time. But it would clearly be intolerable if it set its entrance standards so high as to make a nonsense of the rest of the educational system. Most universities have long since ceased to exercise the right to set their own separate matriculation examinations and have been content to formulate entrance requirements within the framework of the system of school examinations, the standards of which are the ultimate responsibility of the DES—a minor surrender of autonomy which is more than compensated for by the immense practical advantage for universities and schools alike. At present, when entry is competitive and universities can insist on an even higher requirement than their own declared minimum, there is no conflict with public interest; but as places in universities come more nearly to match demand, such halcyon days will pass; and if an easement of the effective entrance standards should result in an increase in the wastage rate, the questions of the standard demanded for a first degree and of the effectiveness of university teaching would undoubtedly be raised.

Happily our universities are not faced with the deeper kind of problem affecting their right to admit or reject students which besets some universities elsewhere. It has become part of our tradition that no discrimination should be shown in favour of or against any student on grounds of sex, religion, race, or politics. Such discrimination flouts an enlightened concept of human rights; it runs counter no less to the entire spirit of a university as an institution dedicated solely to truth and the advancement of knowledge. When a government, as happened in Nazi Germany in regard to Jews, and as is happening in South Africa in regard to coloured people, exercises its legal power and ordains that one or other of these discriminations shall be applied, a university may have no feasible alternative to submission; but as a university it cannot concede the rightness of such action, and by protesting in defence of its own right, it would surely be fighting a battle for all freedom.

Our own attitudes have progressively become more liberal. The earlier and almost unnoticed restriction on the ground of sex was swept away as the higher education of women became a live issue; from the 1870s religious tests disappeared; and in the charters of the newest universities racial and political tests also are specifically forbidden. It is interesting to note that in a formal sense it is the universities themselves which are precluded by the clauses in their charters from exercising these discriminations; but the clauses are there because the universities wanted them there, and any government which wished to impose (say) a political test could do so only by abrogating the charter itself.

2. *The appointment of academic staff.* Here both institutional autonomy and the academic freedom of the individual are involved. That a university should be unrestricted in its appointment of staff, without reference to, or permission from, any other authority, seems to us self-evidently the only sensible way to ensure that the university is well served. In some other countries they think differently. It is only the university which can reach a proper decision on the academic suitability of a man or woman for a particular post; and the intrusion of any other consideration is an irrelevancy. Only in the case of the few Regius chairs at Oxford and Cambridge and in Scottish universities is the formal choice in hands other than those of the universities. For the rest, this freedom of the universities is absolute and unchallenged.

This right of appointment is a vital guarantee to the universities of freedom of thought and expression. To it there is an important corollary. To be effective this right must be supported by reasonable security of tenure; and the statutes of universities now generally contain provisions (including the right of appeal) which preclude dismissal of staff save on grounds of criminal conviction or neglect of duty. A member of staff must be free to pursue the truth of his subject wherever it leads him. In many subjects, if he finds himself in conflict with current opinion, only his fellow experts will be affected.

But there are some more sensitive areas where religious, economic, sociological, or political orthodoxies are involved; and there an academic worker, though expressing views which are within his special field of learning and which have been conscientiously arrived at, may fall foul of a wider public. It is in this kind of situation that a university may be confronted by the displeasure of a government department, the criticisms of parliamentary back-benchers, or an outburst of popular indignation. But the issue is clear: in the exercise of its autonomy, and in the interests of freedom of thought, a university must defend the right of its members to complete freedom of expression on matters within their scholarly competence. Embarrassment sometimes arises when a member of staff expresses unpopular or controversial opinions on matters outside his own field. His rights of expression as a citizen, however, are in no way diminished or enlarged by his official position; but it is not always easy for such a member of staff, however much he tries, to dissociate himself and his university in this kind of context. The university has to shrug its shoulders and let the storm pass.

3. *The determination of the content of university education and the control of degree standards.* It is part of the academic freedom of a university to decide for itself what subjects it will teach, in what way it will present them, and what standard of attainment in any subject or combination of subjects it will require before awarding its degree. It is by the exercise of this right that universities fulfil the important function for the community of maintaining the standards of intellectual excellence; and that is something the community cannot afford to see impaired. The right, however, would clearly be abused if universities took no account at all of the changing needs and desires of society; but the history of (say) the last hundred years shows how well universities have adjusted themselves by expanding their range of studies and the balance between them. It is true that the major changes in favour of science and technology in the last two decades could not have come about without the financial inducements and support of the government; but the important point is that the universities, acting with a strong sense of national responsibility, reached a decision in this matter which was of their own making.

4. *The determination of size and rate of growth.* It is only recently that this aspect of university autonomy has called for comment.

The post-war expansions have raised the question, however, whether too rapid and too great a growth may not destroy for staff and students all sense of belonging to an academic community, and create educational and administrative difficulties which could not be solved without loss of that atmosphere which is part of the life of a university. In this matter the UGC has been most meticulous in its approaches to the universities. The decision is one which necessarily has to be left with each university; for it would be quite impracticable, as well as an infringement of autonomy, to try to compel a university to take more students than it wanted to. The alternative for the university, however, was expounded with feline suavity by the Robbins Committee: 'If, when all the reasons for change have been explained, the institution still prefers not to co-operate, it is better that it should be allowed to follow its own path. This being so, it must not complain if various benefits going to co-operating institutions do not come its way.' The collective response of the universities has on no occasion since 1939 been disappointing. The fact has been faced that the cosy little university of pre-war days has gone for ever. So much has there been a feeling in universities that expansion is inevitable that on some occasions the university response has been in excess of the figures the UGC has had in mind.

5. *The establishment of the balance between teaching, research, and advanced study, the selection of research projects, and freedom of publication.* Teaching and research in a university cannot be put into water-tight compartments, or the balance between them assessed precisely in terms of man-hours and expenditure. It would be futile for government to try to lay down any hard and fast rule, and the matter has virtually to be left to a university's own judgement formed in the light of its responsibility to the community. At a time when every possible place is needed for undergraduates, the universities must expect to be under pressure (as they are) from the UGC and public opinion; but that is a very different matter from denying them the right to exercise their discretion about the way they shall deploy their resources: their practical problem is to adjust the demands of a 'crash programme' to a considered policy for a long-term future.

The selection of research projects is one facet of academic freedom; no topic concerned with the advancement of knowledge is illegitimate in a university; and the question whether the results of a piece of research are likely to be of immediate utility is, as we have said earlier, basically irrelevant. What particular research projects are carried on depends partly on the interests of individuals and departments, and partly on finance; but, within the limits of available funds, there is no interference with a university's choice. Apart from seeing to it that very expensive projects are not unnecessarily duplicated, the UGC places no restriction on the research which is financed out of its block grant.

Freedom of publication is essential to the purposes of a university: access to knowledge must be unrestricted. There are very exceptional circumstances, such as times of war, when in the interests of the community some research must be conducted in conditions of complete secrecy; but normally universities are rightly so jealous of this freedom that they refuse to undertake any research, whether for government departments or industry, the results of which cannot be fully disclosed.

6. *The allocation of recurrent income among the various categories of expenditure.* This has become the most controversial and delicate of all the aspects of university autonomy—indeed the only one about which the universities have any serious reason for concern. As we have previously seen, the UGC and its predecessors have always avoided earmarked grants as far as possible, precisely on the ground that they restricted the freedom of universities. When such grants have been made, the circumstances have been quite exceptional. The universities too have viewed them with misgivings; so much so, that when in 1949 special funds were offered through the UGC to improve academic salaries, one university was on the point of refusing on principle. The practical advantage to the universities of financial autonomy within the block grant is that they have flexibility in taking decisions on needs as they arise, without having to secure permission to transfer sums from one item of their estimates to another; and in view of the complicated considerations often involved in decisions which only the uni-

versity can properly assess, the autonomy tends towards greater rather than less efficiency. In broad terms, the need to balance the university budget is a self-regulating safeguard against over-all waste and extravagance.

But there is also another aspect of the matter: the public control of the spending of public funds—a fundamental principle to which exceptions should be made only for the most compelling of reasons. It is here that the interest of two parliamentary committees is aroused, the Select Committee on Estimates (SCE) and the Select Committee on Public Accounts (PAC). The SCE rarely comments on university affairs; but in July 1965 it made a number of recommendations affecting the structure and secretariat of the UGC, the working of the system of quinquennial grants, and the timing of capital grants.

But it is the PAC which is for the universities the more formidable body. First established by W. E. Gladstone, its function has been said to be 'to put the fear of Westminster into Whitehall'. On several occasions since 1946 it has raised the question whether the Comptroller and Auditor General should have access (and all that is thereby implied) to the records of the UGC and the books of account of the universities. The Treasury itself on each occasion joined issue and defended the immunity of the UGC and the universities from the ministrations of the Comptroller. The situation would appear to be very different now that the UGC is under the aegis of the DES, which, like all other departments of government, has long been accustomed to the procedures of accountability to Parliament through the PAC and the Comptroller. The universities are in fact the only part of the responsibilities of the DES for which it does not have that accountability; and if logicality had complete sway in our affairs, it could be only a matter of time, and that a short one, before the PAC had its way. If—or when—that happens, the universities could count it as a gain that they had a defence against uninformed or malicious criticism of their handling of public funds. It would certainly involve them in irritating and even trivial supervision of their routine accounts; but that is perhaps a price they may have to pay for their wider and more important freedoms. Already in 1965 the UGC began to ask universities for a detailed analysis of departmental costs showing what is expended in terms of money and effort on (*a*) undergraduate teaching, (*b*) postgraduate teaching and supervision, and (*c*) personal research. From the very nature of university work any such apportionment must be largely arbitrary; but the fact that the exercise has been called for seems to indicate the way the wind is blowing.

Healthy relations between the universities and the state must be based on mutual confidence and trust. The importance and validity of university autonomy is that, just as Parliament is the bulwark of civil liberties, so autonomous universities are the bulwark of intellectual liberty and freedom of thought and expression. The diminution of that autonomy in any important particular is in the long run detrimental to the well-being of a democratic society. The universities, on the other hand, are part of that society in which they have their being and they therefore cannot disclaim responsibility to that society. This responsibility has an added force when it is the resources of the state which in so large a measure make their continued existence possible. There may be times when it requires nerve on the part of the state and the community to concede and respect this autonomy. It requires trust on the part of the universities to abate even a little of their traditional rights; and wisdom is called for in interpreting those rights in the light of changing circumstances. If truth and the advancement of learning are the stars by which the universities set their course, a sense of public duty must be their helmsman.

Appendix 1

UNIVERSITIES AND FULL-TIME STUDENTS

(The date in brackets after the name of an institution refers to its foundation as a college)

University	Charter Year	1938–9	1958–9	1963–4	Jan. 1966
Oxford	*(1167)*	5,023	8,699	8,963	9,824
Cambridge	*(1209)*	5,931	8,844	9,170	9,823
London	*1836*	13,191	20,993	23,955	26,454
Imperial College (1907)		1,094	2,541	2,979	3,335
King's College (1829)		1,591	2,105	2,349	2,441
London School of Economics (1895)		1,016	2,062	2,450	2,555
Queen Mary College (1915)		401	1,304	1,431	1,639
University College (1826)		2,162	2,938	3,426	3,751
Guy's Hospital Medical School (1769)		959	1,048	1,005	1,031
Birmingham *(1880)*	*1900*	1,433	3,942	4,982	5,715
Bristol *(1876)*	*1909*	1,005	3,080	4,000	4,718
Durham	*1832*	412	1,398	1,914	2,524
East Anglia	*1964*	—	—	115	807
Essex	*1965*	—	—	—	399
Exeter *(1922)*	*1955*	422	1,232	1,855	2,385
Hull *(1927)*	*1954*	—	1,420	2,243	3,071
Keele *(1949)*	*1962*	—	689	992	1,246
Kent	*1965*	—	—	—	460
Lancaster	*1964*	—	—	—	769

University	Charter Year	1938–9	1958–9	1963–4	Jan. 1966
Leeds (*1874*)	*1904*	1,757	4,538	6,233	6,801
Leicester (*1918*)	*1957*	—	1,053	1,903	2,278
Liverpool (*1881*)	*1903*	2,055	3,667	5,114	5,369
Manchester (*1851*)	*1880*	2,108	4,626	5,908	6,700
M/c. Coll. of Science and Technology (1902)		354	1,487	2,300	2,539
Newcastle (*1871*)	*1963*	1,297	3,556	4,402	4,904
Nottingham (*1881*)	*1948*	582	2,367	3,067	3,857
Reading (*1892*)	*1926*	584	1,425	1,942	2,722
Sheffield (*1879*)	*1905*	767	2,715	3,890	4,543
Southampton (*1902*)	*1952*	268	1,446	2,094	3,039
Sussex	*1961*	—	—	885	2,129
Warwick	*1965*	—	—	—	416
York	*1963*	—	—	220	993
Former CATS					
Battersea (Surrey)	*1966?*	—	—	—	1,745
Birmingham (Aston)	*1966*	—	—	—	2,059
Bradford	*1966?*	—	—	—	2,277
Bristol (Bath)	*1966?*	—	—	—	1,114
Brunel	*1966?*	—	—	—	885
Chelsea†	—	—	—	—	924
Loughborough	*1966*	—	—	—	1,754
Northampton (City Univ.)	*1966*	—	—	—	1,834
Salford	*1966?*	—	—	—	2,351
Total England		**37,189**	**77,177**	**96,077**	**129,428**
Wales University of Wales	*1893*	2,779	5,851	8,261	9,841
Aberystwyth (1872)		663	1,433	1,893	2,113
Bangor (1884)		485	1,143	1,702	2,038
Cardiff (1883)		970	1,819	2,430	2,780
Swansea (1920)		488	1,286	2,069	2,657
Welsh National School of Medicine (1931)		173	170	167	253
St. David's College, Lampeter (*1822*)		—	—	186	266
Former CAT: Cardiff†		—	—	—	1,091
Total Wales		**2,779**	**5,851**	**8,447**	**11,198**

University	Charter Year	1938–9	1958–9	1964–5	Jan. 1966
Scotland					
Aberdeen	*1494*	1,211	1,872	2,768	3,804
Dundee (*1881*)	*1967?*	[*see St. Andrews*]		1,728	2,052
Edinburgh	*1583*	3,205	5,537	6,925	8,292
Glasgow	*1451*	4,175	5,583	6,630	6,983
Heriot-Watt (*1821*)	*1966*	—	—	—	1,047
St. Andrews	*1410*	928	2,418	1,563	1,700
Stirling	*1967?*	—	—	—	—
Strathclyde (*1796*)	*1964*	515	1,766	2,307	4,459
Total Scotland		10,034	17,176	21,921	28,337
TOTAL GT. BRITAIN		**50,002**	**100,204**	**126,445**	**168,963**
N. Ireland					
Queen's, Belfast (*1845*)	*1908*	1,590	2,691	4,126	5,361
Coleraine	*1968?*	—	—	—	—
Eire					
Trinity College, Dublin	*1592*	1,488	2,477	2,886	3,209
National Univ. of Ireland	*1908*	3,643	6,485	9,271	11,105
Dublin (*1851*)		*2,121*	*4,218*	*5,740*	*6,793*
Cork (*1845*)		*853*	*1,275*	*1,947*	*2,262*
Galway 1845)		*669*	*992*	*1,584*	*2,050*

† Chelsea is to be federated with London, and Cardiff with Wales.

Appendix 2

Bibliographical Note

The standard work on mediaeval universities, including Oxford and Cambridge, is: H. Rashdall, *The Universities of Europe in the Middle Ages* (ed. F. M. Powicke & A. B. Emden, 3 vols., 1936). For Oxford see: C. E. Mallet, *A History of the University of Oxford* (3 vols., 1924–7); for Cambridge, J. B. Mullinger, *The University of Cambridge* (3 vols., 1873–1911), and D. A. Winstanley, *Unreformed Cambridge* (1935), *Early Victorian Cambridge* (1940), *Later Victorian Cambridge* (1947). Shorter but useful are: A. Mansbridge, *The Older Universities of England* (1923); J. Wells, *Oxford and its Colleges* (1930 and later ed.); *Handbook to the University of Oxford* (1946 and later ed.); S. C. Roberts, *Introduction to Cambridge* (1934 and later ed.). Many of the individual colleges have published their own histories.

For Scotland we have: J. Kerr, *Scottish Education* (1910); J. D. Mackie, *The University of Glasgow* (1954); A. Grant, *Story of the University of Edinburgh* (2 vols., 1884); A. Logan Turner (ed.), *History of the University of Edinburgh, 1883–1933* (1933).

For London see: D. W. Logan's brief *The University of London* (1956 and later ed.); H. H. Bellot, *University College, London, 1826–1926* (1929); F. J. C. Hearnshaw, *Centenary History of King's College, London* (1929). For Durham see: C. E. Whiting, *The University of Durham* (1932).

The civic universities as a whole are dealt with in: 'Bruce Truscot' (E. A. Peers), *Red Brick University* (1943); W. H. G. Armytage, *The Civic Universities* (1955, a mine of information about all universities and education in general); G. L. Brook, *The Modern University* (1965). For the history of individual universities see: H. B. Charlton, *Portrait of a University* [Manchester] (1951); A. N. Shimmin, *The University of Leeds* (1954); A. W. Chapman, *The Story of a Modern University* [Sheffield] (1955); B. Cottle & J. W. Sherborne, *The Life of a University* [Bristol] (1951); E. W. Vincent & P. Hinton, *The University of Birmingham* (1947); J. Simmons, *New University* [Leicester] (1958); W. M. Childs, *Making a University* [Reading] (1933), by a man who did it; A. C. Wood, *History of the University College of Nottingham* (1953); H. J. W. Hetherington, *The University College at Exeter* (1963).

The aims and structure of the new universities are expounded in: A. E. Sloman, *A University in the Making* [Essex] (1964) and D. Daiches (ed.), *The Idea of a New University* [Sussex] (1964). For Sussex, East Anglia, and York see also: Murray G. Ross (ed.), *New Universities in the Modern World* (1966).

For Wales see: D. E. Evans, *The University of Wales* (1953); and for Ireland: C. Maxwell & K. C. Bailey, *A History of Trinity College, Dublin* (2 vols., 1946–7) and T. W. Moody & J. C. Beckett, *Queen's, Belfast* (2 vols., 1959).

Useful works of a more general kind are: E. Barker, *British Universities* (1946) and J. Duff, *Universities in Britain* (1959)—short but illuminating pamphlets; E. Ashby, *Technology and the Academics* (1958) and *Community of Universities* (1963); R. O. Berdahl, *British Universities and the State* (1959), unsurpassed in its field; Clark Kerr, *The Uses of the University* (1963), an exposition of a modern point of view by the President of the University of California; T. Kelly, *A History of Adult Education in Great Britain* (1962). A. Flexner, *Universities, American, English, German* (1930) is a trenchantly critical survey. The *Universities Quarterly* publishes valuable articles on current topics.

Important and authoritative reports are published quinquennially by the UGC under the title *University Development*, the most recent of which (1964) covers the period 1957–62. The committee's annual *Returns from Universities* is wholly statistical; its *Annual Survey* deals in narrative form with current matters of policy and development. The Association of Commonwealth Universities publishes an annual *Yearbook* containing much detailed information about all universities.

Finally, there is the Report of the Robbins Committee entitled *Higher Education* (1963–4) which, with its appendixes and statistical tables, fills 2,373 pages. The main Report gives a general survey of higher education and makes 178 separate recommendations; Appendix 1 deals with the demand for places; Appendix 2 (in 2 vols.) with students and their education; Appendix 3 with teachers in higher education; Appendix 4 with administrative, financial, and economic aspects; and Appendix 5 with higher education in other countries (including invaluable accounts of universities in Australia, Canada, France, Germany, the Netherlands, New Zealand, Sweden, Switzerland, the USA, and the USSR).

Index